Pain. Process. Purpose.
THE 3 P'S TO FINDING YOUR SPIRITUAL IDENTITY

CHANEL CHASE

PAIN . PROCESS . PURPOSE .

Copyright ©2017 Chanel Chase
Publishing Company: October 7th Publishing LLC

Address:
P.O. Box 1271
Mableton, GA 30126

All rights reserved. No part of this book may be reproduced or transmitted in any form or by any means whatsoever (electronic, mechanical, scanning, photocopy, recording, or any other form) without written permission from the author, except for brief quotations in a book review.

ISBN: 978-0-9994946-0-8

Cover Design: Tamlyn Design

Book Layout: Solex Enterprises, LLC

Editor: Dr. Asheia Wynne

PAIN . PROCESS . PURPOSE .

CHANEL CHASE

~ DEDICATION ~

I dedicate this book to my daddy, Johnny Chase. You have been and will always be the push to my ongoing success. You saw the impact I would make in this world before I saw it. You breathed success into me the day I was born. You watered the seeds of success through tough love and many tears. You watched those seeds begin to bloom because of your constant support in my life. Many people in the world are not blessed with a loving father, and I am thankful for you. The many ups and downs in our relationship have made me stronger, and your ongoing advice kept me grounded. Your words of wisdom and overflow of love have reminded me each day to keep pushing for greater. Thank you for always instilling in us the spirit to think BIG. Today, I stand with one more accomplishment. Because of you, I am doing something that you prophesized over my life many years ago. I am publishing this book that will impact many people. Thank you for the drive that you instilled in me. Thank you for being a loving father. You were not perfect, but you were mine. Thank you for being a loving husband to my mother and living the example of what a true husband should be. You gave me insight on what to expect from my future husband, and that will never be forgotten. You are still holding my hand daily, and every day, I'm realizing how blessed I am to have had you in my life. You will never be forgotten. You will be in my heart forever.

With much love,

Your Baby Girl

ACKNOWLEDGMENTS

First and foremost, thank you God for using me to give a message to each person that picks up this book. This was all of you and none of me. Thank you for the opportunity.

To my Mom,
Words cannot express the love that you have shown me. Thank you for every inch of support you have given me my entire life. Thank you for taking your time to help me along this process. You and Dad have been instrumental in my life and helped me create a foundation to do the "impossible." Thank you for every strategic relationship that you have formed to allow me to achieve this accomplishment, and I appreciate many more years of your love and support. I love you mommy.

To Sterlin Chase,
Thank you for being a good brother. We may fuss and argue, but when you are needed, you are always there. You believe in me, and I appreciate you allowing me to be one of your role models. Thank you for being an amazing little brother. I pray you will have much success. I love you so much.

To Cornell James,
Thank you for believing in me with everything that I do. I appreciate the love that you pour into me, and I appreciate the support that we give each other. Thank you for allowing God to use you to come into my life and taking on the role of my best friend. You have been nothing short of great towards me. I love you.

To Alicia Woods,
Thank you for believing in me every step of the way. From the first time that I told you that I wanted to write a book to the multiple times I sent you pieces to read. Thanks for being an amazing friend. I appreciate your support and constant love. I love you.

To Jameela Pitts,
Thank you for encouraging me to tell my story, and the many long nights we spent up talking about life and the way I felt throughout my journey. I appreciate you sticking with me through the ups and downs of our friendship. Thank you for the constant support. I love you.

To Ebony Rowe,
Thank you for being an awesome friend. Words cannot express the impact you and your family have played in my life. You have been there through many parts of my process, and although our friendship has only been a couple of years, you have played a vital role in my purpose. I love you.

To Janay Brinkley,
Thank you for taking the time to give me advice throughout the process of creating this book. I appreciate your love, encouragement, and support.

To Dr. Asheia Wynne,
Thank you for becoming my editor without any questions, and birthing ideas to make this book amazing.

To Nicole Jennings (We Manage Brands LLC),
Thank you for being an amazing branding specialist, and I thank you and your amazing team for all your help and creative ideas.

To Dr. Jewel Tankard,
Thank you for being an amazing mentor and helping me push myself a little further. I thank your team for assisting in every way. I am honored that you took the time to write the foreword to my book, and I appreciate the consistent love, guidance, and support.

To all my friends and family, especially Brittany Dean, Alexus McCullum, Talisa Cummings, Ashley Woodard, and the entire James Family, Thank you for your constant love and support. I appreciate everything that everyone has done in my life. All of you played a role in this book becoming a real thing instead of a figment of my imagination, so I thank you!

PAIN . PROCESS . PURPOSE .

Table of Contents

DEDICATION	5
Acknowledgments	7
Table of Contents	11
FOREWORD	13
Introduction	15
PART I: PAIN	19
Chapter 1: Lost Identity	19
Chapter 2: Realizing My Downfall	25
Chapter 3: God is Love	33
Chapter 4: Obedience Through Pain	49
Your Intimate Thoughts	57
PART II: PROCESS	61
Chapter 5: Sex, Celibacy, and Obedience	61
Chapter 6: Road to Finding my Identity	71
Chapter 7: Bumpy Roads	79
Chapter 8: Spending Time Alone with God	87
Your Intimate Thoughts	95
Part III: Purpose	99
Chapter 9: Leading Into My Purpose	99
Chapter 10: Realizing God's Greater Purpose	109
Chapter 11: God Has a Plan	117
Chapter 12: Aligning my Purpose with my Spiritual Identity	127
Your Intimate Thoughts	135
Let's Work Through Your Journey Together	139
Let's Keep in Contact	141
About the Author	143

PAIN. PROCESS. PURPOSE.

CHANEL CHASE

FOREWORD

It has truly been an honor to mentor Chanel. She is so bright, energetic, and full of life. She is so hungry for success and willing to adapt and do what it takes to become her absolute best. I have thoroughly enjoyed her teachable spirit, strong dedication, commitment and work ethic. Her book is such a great read. Personally, I understand the necessity of processing through pain. In my previous marriage, I decided to no longer feel sorry for myself. I knew that instead of hosting a never-ending pity party, I needed to take responsibility for my role in the mess I found myself in. I had to grow up, be honest, and not allow that negative situation to destroy my destiny. I would have never gotten to a place of healing without being honest. In this amazing story, hear how this daddy's girl had to really grow up and process her pain to discover her purpose. You won't be disappointed and may even want to use this book for your book club. I highly recommend this book and I'm so proud of her for being so transparent in sharing her story.

Jewel Tankard

PAIN. PROCESS. PURPOSE.

PAIN. PROCESS. PURPOSE.

INTRODUCTION

I remember waking up as if everything had been okay. My life was great. I had a wonderful job, a house, and a loving family. What could be missing? Everything. Everything was missing and nobody could see the pain that I felt on a constant basis. Nobody saw the tears I was crying most nights. All they saw was the glitz and the glamour of "my life". Funny, right? Have you ever stopped to really think about what the average person goes through? Have you looked at your friends and ever saw something that just wasn't right with them? Probably not. Most overlook the people that appear to be happy. Most people would say that anything those people are going through is not important because money is not an issue. I decided to write this book to explain the inner workings of a person that was lost. That person was me. I was lost, and I'm okay to admit that today.

To any person that was left heartbroken after an unhealthy relationship, or any person who has had suicidal thoughts. To the child or widow that has lost their parent or spouse. To the child that has had parental relationship issues, or to any person that is searching for love in all the wrong places. Even to the person that feels alone in life and afraid to express how they feel. To anyone with any relatable emotional issue, this book is for you. This book was written to show you that you are not alone. I feel your journey. I feel your pain. God sees it all. There's an open door at the end of the tunnel.

Throughout the process of being lost, I encountered many phases of life. I went through a phase of pain. That pain birthed a process, and then that process helped me reach my purpose. I found God throughout my journey. I wrote this book to encourage the person that feels like I did, to not give up. It doesn't matter what event took place to get you to where you are. I'm sure that God has a plan for you. I know that sometimes, we try to wear a mask to impress the people around us. Sometimes we are just trying to hide how we feel on the inside because we are ashamed of the emptiness we feel. Don't worry. I've been there.

I've been lost, I've been down, and I've had many issues, but I'm still standing, and so will you. There are many questions that we can ask ourselves everyday about the decisions that we chose to make, but we don't have to. We don't have to beat ourselves up about our past. There is always a lesson to be learned and a testimony to be created. I am going to encourage every person reading this book to decide that you are going to find God in your situation. Not just the "good," but more importantly, the "God." As I share my journey with you, I pray that you are open to examine your own journey. This book is designed for you to evaluate your situation as I tell mine. I will walk you through the details of my pain, my process, and how it led to my purpose. I am opening myself up to you. I am being vulnerable and completely transparent with you, so I pray that you learn to be open and vulnerable with yourself. If no one else can hear you, God can. God showed me through my spiritual journey how He was always there with me.

Throughout this book, I pose many questions for you to think about, and I pray that you take them seriously. I have left pages for you to reflect on your own journey as well. In these pages, please freely write whatever comes to mind. Journaling your thoughts will be a significant part of your process. There is also a workbook that is a companion to this book. If you have the workbook, I will give you specific questions to answer and exercises to complete after you've finished the book to help you with your process. I hope that my journey can impact the life of every person that picks up this book. I pray that you grow closer to God, and you realize that nothing in your life is too hard for God to fix. All things are possible to those that believe.

God Bless and Enjoy!

PART I: PAIN
Chapter 1: Lost Identity

A part of me used to be so closed off, so lost, and so confused. I didn't know which way was forward or which way was backwards. It honestly all just felt wrong. I didn't know what to do, but lately, I've caught myself praying more, fasting for reasons I couldn't tell you, and crying tears of joy when I should be upset. I never once thought that God could come in and start filling a void that had been empty for so long. I thought all I needed was love! I couldn't even begin to tell you what love was, but the beginning of the battle, of course, started with a boy.

Funny that I would say that, right? What story about love doesn't start with a boy? I fell in love in college. Well, what I thought was love. But I now realize that in fact, I was in lust, and I was infatuated. I can now see that I've been in like before, but not love. I remember being talked down to, feeling insecure, crying many nights, pretending to smile, and feeling weak, wearing pretend happiness. I don't think that is love. Well, I know it wasn't love, but I tried to make myself think that it was.

To be honest, I was just happy to have the attention of a tall, dark, and handsome athlete. Little did I know that this was a start to what I would eventually find out to be pain. I thought that he was the best thing in the world. I was lucky, right? I was popular in college, and now, I was dating the "stereotypical athlete." He had very intriguing attributes at first. He was a huge part of Fellowship of Christian Athletes. He was the starting wide receiver on the football team, and the starting center on the basketball team. I thought I had it made. I was happy at the beginning, but eventually it made an awful turn for the worst. This is where I began to realize that I was slowly losing my identity.

Have you ever felt like that? Has there been a time in your life where you felt that your identity had been stolen and you weren't quite sure how to get it back? This was the beginning of a slippery slope down a path that I didn't see coming. I was pretending to be happy. It was a "front." When I clearly saw that the relationship had taken a toll on me, I didn't get out. Honestly, I'd settled in other relationships before. Why did I settle? I settled because I was afraid to be alone. I just thought that you were supposed to have a boyfriend because that's what people do. Some women would call that weak, but I can't. I call it lost. I was LOST, so lost. I didn't know what love was. I didn't know *how* to love. Here I was with a boy, 3 years had passed, and I was planning my future with someone I knew wasn't right for me. Why would I do that? It's because I didn't know my identity. I forgot the power that I possessed inside of me. I allowed myself to be treated lower than I deserved.

It wasn't all bad. It just wasn't right. Argument after argument, screams after screams, tears after tears, and many lonely nights. I knew something wasn't right, but I wasn't ready to face the reality that I was wasting my time. I thought that I could change the situation. I thought that I could make the words "I love you" really mean exactly that. I wanted to make myself feel like love was real. I smiled on the outside but every bit of my insides cringed at every other relationship that I saw succeed. I had become so attached to the concept of "us" that I had forgotten who I was. I think back to then, and I really thought that "in love" meant that I was supposed to endure the many troubled times because we looked happy. I thought I was supposed to wear the mask of happiness. I remember calling my ex repeatedly with no answer. I remember the hurtful nights of being left alone wondering where he was. I remember trying to be helpful, offering my car to him, then later hearing about other females riding in it. I accepted this behavior. I accepted being treated like less than a person.

On my graduation night from college, I met the girl with whom he had been cheating. I graduated valedictorian and made the mistake of thanking him in my speech. Apparently, that speech raised some questions to the female and later she approached me in the club. To be honest, everything seemed to happen in slow motion. He and the girl both told me that he'd cheated on me. I was looking the girl in the face and even then, it wasn't enough for me to leave. I was buried in so much hurt that I realized I just had to keep the outer appearance "perfect." So, my ex and I talked all night, got up together, drove to Georgia and attended my graduation party with my family as if nothing had happened. Deep inside, I was sick to my stomach, but again, I had lost my identity. I didn't know who I was. I was only who he said I was. He said he was doing me a favor. He made me feel like less than a person. But that was only because *I let him*. The crazy thing is all this happened and I still didn't leave. I stayed. It wasn't until 6 months later when I realized that he was still cheating that I decided to leave. I was tired. It took 4 ½ years for me to come to terms with myself and the mask I was wearing. It took me 4 ½ years to accept the reality that my identity had been taken from me and my journey to restoration had just begun.

I knew the first part of my identity search was finding the real definition of love. How could I truly ever understand my journey without going through the phase of true love? What was it that made me make the decisions that I'd been making? Was it that I longed for attention or was it deeper? You would think that the pain that I faced during the relationship was the story, but it wasn't. That really hurt, but the real pain was trying to recover my identity. I needed to discover what true love was, and uncover who I really was. Hiding behind a mask had become the way I chose to live my life. I hid behind sports, friends, and success in school, fake relationships, and even my emotions. I hid behind whatever could make me feel like I was a part of the crowd. Pain does that. Pain disguises itself as many different characters until you are willing to face it head on. Pain pushed me away from God. Most people say that pain should bring you closer, but it didn't. At this moment in my life, I really hated God. I was angry with God. I didn't understand why I had to go through what I did. It felt like my entire world stopped. I felt useless, as if I was nobody without him. Where did my Kingdom purpose go? Who was I before I met him? I didn't know and quite honestly at that time, I didn't care. Pain made me numb.

The pain that I felt with my 4 ½ years of a "relationship" had been flushed down the drain, and I watched him parade around with the girl he cheated on me with as if she was a trophy. All of this was going on while I was trying to keep face, as if it didn't bother me. I was trying to stay masked. I knew that I didn't know my identity. I only knew how to pretend to be happy, when I really felt trapped. It felt like there was no way out. I remember crying and screaming at God for doing this to me and then one day, I heard God ask me, "Are you sure I did this to you? Do you know who you are?"

The funny thing about this is that I really had to sit in my room and think about that. Was I sure that God did this to me? Did I know who I was? At that point, I began to realize that maybe pain would take me through a process that I needed to endure. Did God really do this to me? I began to pray every day. I would cry and scream and ask God for clarity. I would beg for an answer and the only reply I would get was, "Do you know who you are?" Baffled at that question, I wasn't ready to face it so I continued to cry, pray, scream and ask God the same question repeatedly.

PAIN. PROCESS. PURPOSE.

Then one day, I had to face reality. I really didn't know who I was. For the first time in my life, I came to terms with the fact that my identity had been stolen, and I needed to figure out how to get it back. However, I had no idea where to start. Having grown up in church, my first thought should have been to run to God for help, but it wasn't. I was still mad at God. I tried to figure it out on my own, like most people, but that didn't work in my best interest. I remember many lonely nights and many horrible decisions. I didn't seem to be getting any closer to discovering my identity. I started to hang out with different people to see if I could find happiness in them, but that made the situation worse. I was so lost. I was hiding behind the lies of happiness. I was hiding behind the constant partying, and the makeup that was covering every dried tear, every painful night, and every painful memory. I was hiding to avoid the truth that I didn't know who I was. When that didn't work, I began to hide behind the "infamous bottle." I thought that I could get so drunk that I wouldn't have to worry about how I felt on the inside, *empty*. I didn't feel anything. I hid behind my fancy clothes, my success, and my lifestyle. I really was unhappy and I didn't know who I was.

Chapter 2: Realizing My Downfall

I was experiencing the worst pain that anyone could feel. The pain was seeping in day by day because I lost my identity and misconceived it as love. It wasn't love; it was indeed lust. It was the lust of being wanted, it was the lust of fitting in, and it was the lust of not wanting to be alone. When people think about lust, they think about sexual desires, but you can lust after someone's companionship. I lusted so much that I became everything that he breathed into me. Every word that he said about me, I imagined it to be true. *"I wasn't pretty enough. I was lucky to be with him, and any other girl would love to be with him."* These were all things that he'd told me. I remember the times that he insisted that I wore makeup because the girl before me wore her makeup a certain way. I was falling into a web of hurt and a life under his control, but it wasn't his fault. It was mine.

There had been a void in me for a very long time. I kept meeting guy after guy attempting to "fall in love." Even after all I had been through, I had become accustomed to that false interpretation of "love." I was so angry with God. Why didn't He show me *Real Love?* Where was He when I couldn't make it alone? **Where was He?** Have you ever felt like you needed God and felt like He wasn't there? The truth is that God had been with me the entire time. I just had my back turned away from Him. I started walking in the wrong direction. I blamed God when all He really wanted to do was heal me. I'd been afraid to be different than my peers. I longed for *"what I thought was love,"* but I knew if I was *"different"*, people would not like me. People would disown me. People would make fun of me. Honestly, they already were making fun of me. They were already talking about me, so why not be different? I wanted God to tell me what my next steps were, and explain to me how to love. But truthfully, **how could I learn to love someone else when I didn't even love myself?** I was angry, bitter, hurt, insecure, and unaware of my value. I just hid behind my beautiful smile so people could only see my exterior, but if they were to look into my heart, people would see how cold, bitter, and dead it really was. Has anyone ever felt that way? I was hiding behind the idea of love instead of finding what it really meant. I was willing to morph into who he wanted me to be instead of embracing who God intended me to be.

I couldn't love because I didn't know love. I thought that loving people and having care so deep for people was enough to understand love. I loved bringing joy and smiles to others faces, but only because I longed to be just as bright as their smiles appeared on the outside. I was hiding my identity while trying to live in theirs. I tried to fake love, but I couldn't fake what was in my heart. I was **empty, dead, cold, and bitter.** I was withering away day by day. It wasn't his fault. I allowed myself to believe in the person he wanted me to be, even if it was substandard to what I knew God wanted for me. I let him do it. I gave him my mind and thought that it was okay to jeopardize who I was as a person to become who he needed me to be as a potential mate. I gave up the power of me, and then I forgot what I possessed as a person. Remember when I stated I grew up in church? It was easy for me to justify what I was doing by scripture. That is what happens when you are twisted but gifted, blessed but a mess. I made the scriptures fit what I wanted them to be. I remember nights crying and saying "God you told me *you would never put more on me than I could bear.*" I remember screaming, *you are my help and my redeemer.* I tried to make my mess make sense, but it didn't. That was pain.

I remember going on vacation with my girls and this is where I realized pain had won. It had been two years since I'd started searching for my identity. I was in New Orleans for a New Year's trip with my friends, and for the very first time, the 4 ½ years of my identity loss caught up with me. I remember crying, screaming, and getting drunk. I was at the balcony on the 7th floor of a hotel about to jump off screaming that I couldn't take it anymore. It took four of my friends to calm me down and pull me back to reality. I was willing to take my life. Yes, I was intoxicated, but have you ever heard the saying, *a drunk mind speaks a sober spirit?* That was the truth. I contemplated leaving this earth because I allowed pain to win. Many people will read this and say that girl is crazy, and honestly, looking back, I see that I was. But, I was also lost. Have you ever felt that way? Don't be ashamed. This was a lesson that created a turning point in my life. I let Satan completely seep in, and I didn't see him coming.

I was overwhelmed with life enough to end it without thinking. A boy didn't bring me to that point. My situation influenced it, but I let it get that far. I was letting Satan win. I thought I was hurt, but **no**, my identity was stolen and since I laid it down to Satan, he had every intention of taking it. If it wasn't for God, I'd be dead. At 23 years old with all the potential in the world, I'd be dead because I let Satan win.

At that moment, when I gained consciousness of what was going on, I realized that I was at the lowest point of my life. No one knew until that point, but that night it was very evident to the four friends I was with that my pain was deeper than me just being hurt. I realized that when I looked in the mirror that I didn't recognize myself. Has anybody gotten to that point to where they have no idea about the person they'd turned into? The problem was on the outside, I looked as if I was well put together, but inside, I was torn apart. The best part about being at your lowest point is that there is nowhere to go except to go up. That's what I began to focus on. I got on my knees, for the first time, and cried to God with an open and honest heart. I laid everything down. I truly *casted my burdens onto God so, he could sustain me (Psalm 55:22 KJV)*. Why not? I tried my own way, and it didn't seem to be working. It's sad that God had to be my last option, but I eventually started heading in the right direction. However, it was not easy. During this time, I would talk to God, and I asked him, **"Why would you allow me to get to this point if you loved me as your child?"** I remember that specific conversation so vividly, and He told me that He never chose for me to take this journey. When I made the decision to take this journey, He adjusted my plan.

I remember sitting in my bed baffled. Why didn't God clearly tell me the guy wasn't for me? Why didn't He guide me down the right path? I remember all those questions and fury began to come into my heart. Then God told me, *"I did tell you, but you didn't listen."*

I cried that entire night. I shut God out even further than before because **I blamed Him** for allowing me to encounter this situation. I now know that the reason I went through it was because I walked off the path He created for me. I created my own path. Yes, God knew my steps and the steps that I would take, but they were not the steps that He ordered. Please read the sentences I just wrote carefully. Many people have heard that God orders our steps before we even know them. This is completely true, but what we must realize is that when we do not stay in the will of God and go off and create our own path, we are no longer following the steps that God has ordered. We are simply re-writing our destiny the way **we** created it and not the way that **He** planned for us.

We, as Christians, can always return to the path that He created for us at any time. However, we will probably come back with bruises, scrapes and scars that we would have never encountered had we stayed in God's Will. What I had to truly realize is that what I went through was not a punishment from God, but a self-created detour due to my lack of obedience. For me, that was a hard pill to swallow. Being in the will of God and experiencing His love is something that we can all encounter, but it takes true discipline to be able to fight our flesh and cling to God. That's the only way to fill the voids that the world tells us can only be filled by drugs, alcohol, worldly love, sex and whatever else the world offers. It takes discipline to go through hell and remain steadfast on God. It takes discipline to wait patiently to find love in God while "feeling unloved by man". It takes discipline to earn the money you desire but don't want to work to obtain. Everything in this world, even spiritually, takes consistency and discipline.

Before, I was so lost and confused. I wanted my void to be filled by people and things that were incapable of fulfilling them. I was living my life much differently than the Bible. I had loving parents that could have mentored me on relationships, but I chose to try it my own way. I had a church that I could have attended, but I didn't. I chose to treat God's way of living as if it wasn't a priority. I would eventually get around to doing better. Reality was that my mess would have never been created if I first would have listened to the message that God had destined for me. I just needed to listen. I needed to be *swift to listen, slow to speak, slow to anger (James 1:19 KJV)*. That's biblical. But instead, I was quick to speak and get angry before I even listened to God. Why? Because I was afraid of what He was going to say. I was afraid that He was going to tell me to leave my relationship. That's why I kept walking in the wrong direction asking for His right guidance. Sounds disturbing, right? I was walking the wrong way but still asking God to bless me. I just knew that I would get blessed if I was going the right way, but I wanted my way to be the **RIGHT** way.

There are so many times that I have had this battle in my head. When I was going the wrong way, there was no way God could have blessed me the right way because I was not in the direction He destined me to go. It all is a Godly defined order and sometimes we miss the mark. We are humans. That is why Christ died on the cross; however, when we miss the mark, we can't expect the results to be the same as if we stayed on the path. Our job as Christians is to remain so focused on God that we don't even see the path to create for ourselves. I blamed God for the hurt I'd experienced for 2 years after we broke up. I was angry, but God showed me that He still cared and loved me over the course of the four and half year relationship and the other two years I hated him for putting me through it. Now that is love. For six and a half years, I didn't listen. I was disobedient. I was spiteful, angry, dramatic and ignored God, and guess what? God still loved me.

PAIN . PROCESS . PURPOSE .

PAIN
PROCESS
PURPOSE:
THE 3 P'S TO FINDING YOUR SPIRITUAL IDENTITY

Chanel J. Chase

— CHANEL CHASE —

Chapter 3: God is Love

One day, God revealed to me why I went through that pain. I turned around and began to find my way back to the right path. On the way, I just saw God's hands stretched towards me with His open loving arms waiting on me. That is *love*. He never made me feel worse than I already felt about the decisions I'd made. Instead, He gave me an "understanding" about what happened. He explained that He still loved me despite the past situations. That is a love that cannot be cloned or faked. That is unconditional love. This is where I started to find love. Every painful piece in this masterpiece was important. They each remind me of the love God has for me. When I think of every bad memory in my relationship, I now see the love God was showing me and the process of replacing my hurt with His love. I never experienced a love so deep. I never knew the definition of love until I came into a deeper place with God, praying on my face. In that place, I realized that *He would never leave me or forsake me (Hebrews 13:5)*. I had to believe that. Nobody needed to teach me value. I simply needed to open the bible and God would show me strong women like Ruth to help me understand my worth.

True **love** is found only in God. That revelation was extremely hard for me to grasp. I didn't understand that love could go beyond happiness on Earth. Love can run so deep that even amid mess you find peace. I prayed each day for this love to grow in me. I prayed not to feel weak. I prayed for God to fill my emptiness with only His Word. I prayed consistently, and I began to experience and see what love was for the very first time. I realized that God loves me through my pain, through my suffering, through my bad decisions, through my bad attitudes, and through my arguments. HE STILL LOVES ME. The crazy thing is that I was expecting ungodly people to produce indescribable love. However, only God could see through my faults, and still love me unconditionally.

Have you ever tried to replace God? As I began to dig deeper into what God wanted for me, I realized that **only** God could give me a love that could not be erased. That's why it is so important to die to yourself and give your life to God. It is one thing to say it, but to truly live surrendered to God is a totally different situation. I was on a search for love, and I found God. This brought me to the revelation that God is love. Love is God, and the two cannot coincide without each other. They are one in the same. I also realized that as I had begun to prepare myself for my future husband, it was important that I build a true genuine relationship with God. One that would be edifying to my mind, body, and spirit. One that could identify the fraudulent spirits disguising themselves as something good. I made it seem like I was happy-go-lucky and everything was okay. However, deep inside I was killing myself day by day. My identity was being revealed and I didn't like it. I was unhappy, hurt, frustrated, unloved, empty, and in need of some true guidance. It was not until I focused on God that I began to see what love is and how important it is to love and know God. I was beginning to understand a God-sent man would not only physically see me but also see me spiritually through God's eyes, as one body, one flesh. Love can be so deep, yet so simple. God is Love. Love is God. It is so important to continue to love every single day. I had to adjust going forward. When something happened in my life, I had to be able to identify the difference between what was and wasn't love. Love is God and anything else not associated with God's kind of love is Satanic. God is love.

At that point, I realized that all that I'd experienced was not the guys' fault. It wasn't God's fault. It was my fault. It was my lesson. It was my experience. At that point, I realized that God gave me a choice and I chose to go the other way. I remembered the story of the prodigal son from the bible. The prodigal son was given everything by his earthly father, yet he still left the nest and went out and made horrible choices. He went and wasted everything that he had. As a result, he became truly poor, with no money, food, or possessions. The bible states, *"He longed to fill his stomach with the pods that the pigs were eating, but no one gave him anything (**Luke 15:16 NIV**)."* He truly had nothing. He made bad decisions that cost him everything. Had he just stayed home with his father, he would have been the ruler over their estate. His family was rich. So, he decided to go back home. He knew that his father would not accept who he had become, but he faced his fears anyway. The bible reads, *but his father saw him and was filled with compassion for him; he ran to his son, threw his arms around him and kissed him. The son said to him, Father I have sinned against heaven and against you. I am no longer worthy to be your son. But the father said to his servants, Quick! Bring the best robe and put it on him. Put a ring on his finger and sandals on his feet. Bring the fattened calf and kill it. Let's have a feast and celebrate (**Luke 15:20-22 NIV**).* After remembering this story, I realized I was a prodigal daughter. God had a specific plan for my life. At the beginning of the plan, I had an identity that was tied to a purpose. While He was leading me to that purpose, the journey that I had to face was far more difficult because I went off and squandered away my identity. I was lost without an identity and had become a person that was not tied to my God intended purpose. I was tied to Satan.

God wanted so much more for me. However, the way I began to get reconnected to my purpose was by going back and grounding myself in my identity. That was painful, and I didn't know where to begin. God told me, "You have been wearing masks for a long time and for me to connect you to your purpose, we have to get rid of all the identities of the people that you chose to encounter on your path. You morphed into them and took on the weight of their emotions. You encountered the pain, and the frustrations of life when that was not your journey. It was the journey you chose to go through, but we still have a plan for your purpose, and it will be a different process." At that point, I realized that what I needed to do was to find myself, but this time I would need to find myself in God.

I wasn't quite sure where to start. I honestly had forgotten how to really connect with God. I had ignored and run from God's still, small voice for so long that I couldn't even recognize it. I had allowed Satan to become me, and I was only used to hearing the voices of demons. They made sure I didn't hear God. But something in my heart told me to keep asking God how to hear Him. I would say, " Where do I go to hear you?" I remember one night having a dream that literally took my breath away. I woke up and I really could not breathe. I remember seeing Satan's face in my room and his demons coming to take me. I woke up attempting to scream, but I could not breathe. I remember Satan telling me that I would be with him forever, and for the first time, I felt like I knew what to do. I literally began to try to talk and I muttered out the words, "Jesus HELP!" That dream is so real to me. I remember the day that Satan was trying to pull me away from God altogether, but I called for Jesus and He helped me. I can remember waking up that morning and getting on my knees to pray. I went to the Jabez prayer that my parents used to make me say every day. *Oh, that you would bless me indeed, and enlarge my territories, that Your hand would be with me, and that You would keep me from evil, that I may not cause pain (1* **Chronicles 4:10 NKJV**). That night I discovered my identity was with God. I chose a team. I made sure that I was on the right team this time. God's hand was with me, and that night, He most certainly kept me from evil. Have you ever been faced with a situation where you had to choose God or Satan? I would compare this experience to making a choice between what you know is right versus doing what everyone is doing though it may not be right. It is in these moments that you find your identity in God.

I found my identity was with God, and then I began to ask him to show me who I was. It sounds cliché, but that is real. I came to terms with the fact that I would live a life surrendered to God. I asked God to help me stick with my choice. Usually, when trouble comes people do not notice that they are not with God. However, at your lowest point, you have to choose God's way or the other way. I chose God. From that day on, I began to attend a church. Many days, I sat in church uncomfortable about what was being said because I didn't know who I was. I knew that I was with God, but I was waiting on Him to reveal to me more about myself. I asked God to begin to place the right people in my life for that time in my life. I began to lose friends. I began to lose people that I thought were with me for a lifetime, and I would ask God why I was losing them. I told God about the pain of losing these people. He would simply tell me to trust Him.

I didn't understand at that time, but I now realize that my identity was more important than the people that I was around. I realized doing God's Will was more important than going back down the drain with Satan. I was choosing an identity with God. This is where I learned to trust. Trusting God was a big part of my transformation of discovering my God given identity. The bible instructs us to, *Trust in God with all your heart and lean not to your own understanding* (**Proverbs 3:5-6 NIV**) After losing so many friends, I remember asking God why He would take so much from me since I'd already lost so much. He then reminded me of (**Matthew 16:25 KJV**), *For whosoever will save his life shall lose it and whosoever will lose his life for my sake shall find it.* I was losing everything, but it was okay because I knew that I needed to find my identity in God. I was hungry enough to stick with the process. It hurt to see the people that I loved leaving me. Unfortunately, they were not tied to my purpose or to my God given destiny. I was starting to understand that sometimes it meant that I had to give up the things of comfort to go where God originally designed for me to go. God was showing me that my identity required a calling and sometimes a calling requires elevation to a different realm. This process taught me that elevation requires some separation from people, things, habits, and lifestyles. I realized my identity with God was more important. I knew it wouldn't be easy, and I would face obstacles, but I was ready for the new journey.

What came next? Honestly, everything just fell into place. My life got better. My self-esteem shot right up to the sky. My faith was stronger than ever, and I was just doing the dang thing. Truthfully, I began to encounter test after test after test, and then when I thought it was over, another test came. Because of all the challenges, it could be certainly easy for me to slip back into that sad place. As soon as it seems that you are in a great place, Satan and his army attacks. Honestly, in my life, this is where my mind was attacked. It seemed like the more I searched for peace and the deeper I tried to dig into God's Word, the more negative things would happen. I searched and searched for answers but when I went through my mind I couldn't decipher between the words and the "Word". The problem was I was trying to go to battle with Satan without my armor. In ***Ephesians 6:10-18 (AMP)*** it states, *"Put on God's whole armor {the armor of a heavy-armed soldier which God supplies}, that you may be able {successfully} to stand up against {all} the strategies and the deceits of the devil. For we are not wrestling with flesh and blood {contending only with physical opponents}, but against the despotisms, against the powers,* *against {the master spirits who are} the world rulers of this present darkness, against the spirit forces of wickedness in the heavenly (supernatural) sphere. Therefore, put on God's complete armor, that you may be able to resist and stand your ground the evil day {of danger}, and having done all {the crisis demands} to stand {firmly in your place}.* That means that you can't go into the battle unequipped. To be equipped, we must stand on God's Word. You must have His word so engraved in your heart that when something goes wrong, you can't help but to speak out His Word. That is the only way that you defeat the enemy during his attack on your life. The devil began to attack my mind, and when that did not work, he began to infiltrate my life. By infiltrating my life, he would be able to infiltrate my mind. At the same time that I was digging deeper into God's Word and becoming stronger, Satan began to affect my relationships.

One of the most important relationships that I have in my life is the relationships with my parents, and this is what Satan came to kill, steal and destroy. On Christmas of 2014, my dad and I probably got into one of the biggest arguments that I think could have taken place. The sad part is after the argument took place, I couldn't even begin to tell you how it even started. I can tell you, however, that it was a moment that I would never forget. It was a significant milestone in my life, but I just didn't know that yet. After the argument, I apologized for my part and tried to open the lines of communication with my father but of course that didn't work. This is just how Satan works, it was as if because he couldn't get to my mind, he was trying to get me back to the place I had been for the past 6 ½ years. He wanted me back in a place of searching. Months and months passed and I hadn't spoken to my father. Seriously, I would reach out to him, but there would be no reply. I would try to go home to my parents' house, but there was no communication. It was literally breaking me inside. I even felt myself putting my dad's love before God's love. I know that sounds deep, but I longed to be loved by my dad more than anything at that time. The hole that I had begun to let God fill was now becoming emptier and emptier every day. I was longing for a love from my physical father rather than my spiritual father. I was letting this period of silence pull everything out of me and instead of replenishing my soul with God's Word, I began to fill my heart with worry, hate, anger, and disgust. I was slipping back to where I didn't want to be. Now, I was on the search for love again. Every time my father rejected me, I replaced it with the love that I thought someone or something could give me.

I'm sharing this with you because feelings of emptiness and hurt can be hard to deal with. It is especially difficult to handle these feelings when you lack confidence. I began to date random people because they flattered me. They gave me attention that I desired. It felt good, but this attention was coming from the wrong place. To be completely honest, no one should be able to flatter you because everything that they tell you should be things that you already know. God shows us our value in HIS WORD. That's where your confidence should come from, not other people's words. When somebody flatters you, you are putting their words higher than God's Word. You must be confident in who and whose you are. That is the only way you can succeed in any attack from

Satan. I learned the hard way. As I was saying, I was dating any person who was flattering me, and I was becoming friends with anybody who could see the good in me. Why? Because I did not love myself and I did not seek love from the only person that could fill my emptiness. My dad hadn't communicated with me and our relationship didn't exist anymore, but this is what Satan used to infiltrate my mind and get me off focus. He used my dad as a tool to lower my self- esteem and say negative things about the person I am. He allowed the people who I loved the most to be the ones that were planting negative seeds in my life. These seeds were telling me that I wasn't good enough, that I couldn't be loved, that I was part of the unlovable and that I would never be happy. All these seeds began to uproot my life, and **I watered them every day with my negativity and my unhappiness.** I allowed Satan to come into my life and infiltrate my mind using the tools of the people that I longed to receive love from. He used my family to plant seeds of negativity. You truly must put on the whole armor of God and be prepared for what the devil is going to use to distract you. His sole purpose in life is steal, kill, and destroy *(**John 10:10 KJV**).* He doesn't want to see us happy, and for me to be broken with low self-esteem and no confidence had him smiling. All along I was falling into Satan's plan as he used the people around me. Have you ever thought that the people in your life may be the ones blocking you from reaching the success God has destined for your life? Satan can see weakness, and he will use anyone and anything to infiltrate the peace that God has ordained for your life.

My life was deteriorating as I was letting all the seeds that the devil used my father to plant in me grow. Like the earlier situation, I allowed my inability to be obedient to what God says stray me off my path. Even when obstacles that hurt us appear in our life, we must have enough "Word" in us to still praise through the situation. See, praise welcomes the Lord into the atmosphere, but disobedience welcomes the devil. I say that because I was disobedient and the Lord had already told me to focus on Him no matter what. He would show me His love and begin to fill all my voids. He didn't say, when the devil throws something at you, you can stray away and then come back. He told me to stay focused on Him. See, if my eyes were steadfast and focused directly on Him and moving forward, I wouldn't have been able to see the things that the devil was trying to distract me with. I would have had tunnel vision that was only focused on getting to God so that He could deal with my internal storm.

My problem was love. I needed love. Satan knew that taking my father out of my life would make me feel unloved, but at some point, I needed to be reminded that God is love. So even when earthly people were trying to get me off track and unfocused, I needed to know that only God could fill those holes and only God could love unconditionally. That was the battle I was facing in myself. I thought parents were supposed to have an unconditional love for their children, but you know I had to realize that they too are only humans, and that God is the only person that can always love you. Consequently, for me to feel His love and be acquainted with His love, I had to know His love. The only way to know His love is to know Him. I came to the realization that regardless of if my physical father showed me his love or not during this season, I knew my spiritual father loved me. Sometimes, you must go through a season where you feel alone so that when God brings you out of that season, you will know that it was Him and Him alone that helped you. Humility is birthed from humiliation, and I do not necessarily mean public humiliation. I was internally humiliated that my earthly father was disgusted with me so much that he could not speak to me. I was hurt and upset and felt like the pieces of love that I thought I had were no longer there. Then God showed me after falling off and getting back on track again that He still loved me regardless. I began to see that if I was going to be loved by anybody, I first had to love Him. He was going to teach me how to remain constant in loving myself and others and it first started with Him.

So how do we grow in our relationship with God? Love is found in any friendship, relationship, marriage, or bond and a spiritual relationship with God works the same way. Before we can find His love, we must first know Him. The only way to know God is to read his word and spend time with him. (***Joshua 1:8 KJV***), *this book of the law shall not depart out of thy mouth, but thou shalt meditate day and night and observe to do all that is written. When you do that you will make your way prosperous, and you will have good success.* We cannot treat God as if he is our sidekick. No, God should be first and foremost and our actions should demonstrate that. The same way you wake up in the morning and want to speak to your parents, children, boyfriend, or girlfriend, you should want to wake up and talk to God. God will give you the desires of your heart but you must put some effort into the relationship. This is not a one-sided relationship where He does all the work, He gives you what you want, and then you ignore Him all the time. If the roles were reversed, you would not be a happy camper. God is the same way. He longs to spend time with His children. The more time we put into getting to know Him, the more He reveals His love for us and internally shows us how to love ourselves. No person on this earth should be able to strip your confidence or ruin your self-esteem because our value is mapped out right in God's Word. We are fearfully and wonderfully made by Him **(Psalm 139:14 KJV)**. Now if you don't believe God about your value, how can you believe someone else's opinion? Our value runs deeper than what man can see or say. Our value is God ordained and cannot be stripped by anything. For us to reach a point of value in our lives, we first must create an ear to hear what God is telling us. That begins with developing the Holy Spirit within us.

I was onto something. For the first time in a long time, I felt like God was pushing me in the right direction and I **was listening**. I was seeking His voice. I found it because I wanted to hear it. If you ever get to a point where you can't hear God, it's because we are not seeking to hear Him. *Ask and it will be given to you; seek, and you will find, knock and it will be opened to you* **(*Matthew 7:7 NKJV*)**. I remember sitting and getting this revelation for the first time. I remember not understanding at first. Then I came to understand that what I went through was not always God's intentional design. However, if we follow Him, He will provide. Tamela Mann says it best in her song, "God Provides." It is true that we shouldn't worry because God will always be there even when we don't think that He is. When I couldn't hear God's voice, I wasn't listening to His voice. I didn't want direction. I wanted to try to figure it out on my own, and that got me nowhere. I was lost, but as I began to discover my God given identity, I was becoming more and more like God. I really felt like no matter the circumstance, He would provide.

Losing friends was a big deal to me. I know it seems silly, but it was a test in finding my identity. Some I lost for unknown reasons, and some I lost because I began to **change**. They said I was acting different, or they felt we didn't have similar interest. I didn't understand why God had all these people falling out of my life, but my goal was to try to trust God. I knew it wasn't easy, but it was worth it. I began to cry and ask God, why He was continually taking people away from me, and He began to reveal the truth to me piece by piece. This time, I was listening. I had my ear gates set to receive what God had for me. He then began to show me that the people that were leaving were only leaving for a season and that season was coming to an end. My identity was slowly beginning to be revealed. Baffled by this, I asked God for help. Why didn't I know exactly who I was? Then He gave me the revelation of the layers.

He told me to think about a diamond and how it begins as a decaying plant, and carbon that becomes coal. Everybody looks at the coal as a dark, ugly, dirty, black blob, but they don't know what's underneath. However, when people begin to apply heat, it uncovers layer after layer, and eventually many layers down, they find something remarkable, a diamond. I was like that coal. I started off as a decaying person, attached to the wrong things and the wrong people. I became stubborn, angry, and mad at God. I blocked Him out. Like the coal, my heart was a dark, ugly, dirty, black blob. I began to listen to God and we applied some heat to Satan and some layers of my hardened heart began to fall off. Some of the masks I was wearing began to fall off and who I was becoming didn't align with the people who were attached to me. I didn't fit in with them anymore because I was moving forward in discovering my identity. Sometimes, the very thing we are trying to hold onto is what is keeping us from finding our purpose and identity in God. I began to listen to God. I was getting closer to my purpose, and I wasn't as hurt by those seasonal friends leaving my life. I trusted God to bring the right things and people to my life. This was the first phase of becoming a diamond. I was finally listening to God. However, to find my identity, I needed to do more than just listen to God. I needed to obey Him. On the other side of my obedience, I knew was going to be my provision.

Chapter 4: Obedience Through Pain

Listening was hard enough, but obeying became even harder. I remember thinking to myself, God are you sure I'm just supposed to sit back and let all these people leave my life? I felt lonely. I was at a point where I had gotten so comfortable with the mask that revealing myself began to seep in and I remember Satan trying to distract me from where I was supposed to be getting too. It was hard. Losing friends was never easy, but I kept being reminded that my identity was more important. I would ask God if I could call people, and I would hear NO. I would tell him that I missed my friends, but I remember hearing, "stop acting like you need people when you only need me". Then I was put to the ultimate test. *Disobedience won. Disobedience played one of the main roles in the situation with my dad.* I remember spending Christmas with my family one year. Reminiscing on the situation, it was the first Christmas in my house that I purchased, and my family came and stayed with me. My dad and I were getting along, and then suddenly what was a calm family holiday turned into World War III. We were screaming and yelling at each other, and I remember God whispering in my ear and saying cease, but I didn't. I kept going because my feelings were more important. I failed the test. I began to let the pain (Satan) win. I began to let what was going on with me and my lost identity affect my family. Our family unity was destroyed because of my disobedience. What I thought was a one night argument turned into a 9-month complete silence between my dad and me. Who wouldn't be mad? I was mad again, but this time not at God.

I was mad at myself. It wasn't God that caused the problem; it was me and my disobedience.

I didn't realize it had consequences as big as what had happened. Here I was on my journey to discovering my identity, and I allowed Satan to corrupt the journey. Furthermore, this time I did it with my eyes open. Not only did I have friends not talking to me, I had a father who I loved very much not talking to me. I looked at this situation and I asked God many times, was I the problem? What was wrong with me? Would I ever get back to who He wanted me to be? And I remember Him telling me, "Although the journey may be long, you will get there." It brought a little comfort knowing that God was with me, but I knew that the journey I was facing would get harder.

Not knowing what masks were going to come off next, and who I was turning into began to bother me. I didn't know if I was getting closer to God or further away. I remember becoming so overwhelmed and hurt in my room one night that I just cried. I asked God many times, why do I feel so alone if I'm doing the right thing? Why do I keep praying about things that aren't changing? My dad wasn't talking to me, I could count my friends on one hand, and the life that I once knew was completely gone. Nothing seemed to be going right. I remember hearing God ask me, "How did I expect to get things right if I was not going to be obedient to what He told me to do?" It was at that point that I realized that I was listening to God lead me, but I was not trusting God to take over my life completely. I wouldn't relinquish the control.

Most Christians think the same way; they don't fully trust God enough to give Him control of their lives. I thought that I was trusting God with my relationships, friendships, and everything else, but I realized that I was just controlling them. Anything that fit my plan for my life, I would say that it was God, and anything that didn't fit my plan, then I didn't want to acknowledge it. I was controlling my own life, but I was allowing everyone to think that God was controlling it. I was unhappy with my dad, and I was unhappy with my past relationship. Truthfully, all I had to do was trust God, relinquish control to Him, and wait on Him to fix it. That's part of unmasking our identities in Christ.

I knew that **my way on this journey would not work.** It couldn't work because without God, I was lost. I didn't know what it meant to do everything that God told me to do without hesitation no matter what I felt on the inside. It was a journey to finding my identity. I finally had begun to realize that I wasn't by myself in the journey. It was my journey with God. Even though emotionally I felt all my friends and close family were distant or no longer in my life, I was learning that God would fill that void. I couldn't keep running. I was consistently running, hiding, and being lost. I was hiding behind me. I was scared to unveil the person that I was because I didn't want to be obedient to that still, small voice in my head. It was the one that I was supposed to listen to through every journey but didn't. I had been trying to run from rejection, hurt, pain, and so much more that I honestly ended up losing myself through those very things I was running from. The same things that I thought would be the breath of my life were the very things that killed my identity. I buried God under every worry that I had so I was forced to ignore the voice to obey. I allowed my thoughts and what I wanted to take precedence over God's plan, and that is why I lost the many things that I thought were important.

I didn't even listen to God about the people that I should and shouldn't have been associated with. I began to form all sorts of relationships with people because I was trying to fill voids that were so deep within me that I couldn't see the true reason for my actions. I had many great relationships with great people that were ruined because I tried to make my plan, God's plan. I was learning that I couldn't have that control if God was going to use me. I was going to need to obey what He told me to do in every area of my life. I wanted to choose. I wanted to do one thing around one group of people, and then I wanted to trust God around other people. I had split identities, and where God was getting ready to take me required me to get on one accord with finding myself. I lost myself because of disobedience. I knew I didn't want to be there again, but all I could think about was what other people would think about me. I think that is where Satan began attempting to trap me back into captivity. When I began to think about branching away from some of the normal activities that the people I was hanging around did, I thought about being different and losing the "relationships we had." My delayed obedience caused the delay in my breakthrough.

Has there been a time in your life where God told you that a season was over with someone and you stuck around? That is where I was in life. I was sticking around people, situations, and things that I had no business around because I knew my season was up. However, I wasn't ready mentally for what I knew God was preparing me for. I didn't even have the courage to obey God and see if I did. Most people would say that I was crazy, but to put things in perspective at this point in my life, I had already been hurt by what I thought was love. My dad and I were not getting along, and the only thing I had left was my friends, and God was telling me that my season with those friends was over.

I didn't listen. I continued to stay parked on stupid and stuck on dumb, not listening to anything that God was telling me. The problem was He was blessing me with the people that were going to push me to the next level, but I wasn't ready because I allowed seasons to outweigh their welcomes. That was due to disobedience. I was being blessed with the right relationships but couldn't see the value in them because I was still lost in the others pretending to be someone that I wasn't, and it was allowing me to dig a deeper hole in my life than necessary. But it was a lesson I was creating for myself. I was creating a cycle of having one foot in the world and one foot stuck with God. *A double minded man is unstable in all his ways* (**James 1:8 KJV**). That's where I was, unstable. I wanted to fit in with the crowd, but I also wanted to do God's Will. But what I realized was I needed to separate myself in order to handle the next level of where I was going.

Sometimes, we deny God until we are backed into a corner and have no other choice, but to go towards God. The new relationships that God was putting in my life began to pull me to a place where I had to make a choice to follow God or to stay in the world. This was my chance at obedience. But I still didn't listen. I tried to dabble with both. I wanted my unyoked friends to go to the next level with me, but that wasn't their purpose for my life. I slowly began to lose not just the unyoked friends, but the friends that were also sent for a higher purpose. My disobedience had again left me alone. It was then that I realized change had to take place. I felt alone. My dad wasn't talking to me. I lost friends. I wasn't in a relationship. I didn't even know who I was, but I knew I needed God. I had to think back to every situation that I had been through and realize that God had never left. He was holding my hand through every situation, so if He was doing it before, He was still doing it. It was up to me to make a conscious decision that it was going to be me and God and that I would try not to let anything else come between us. Have you ever been in that position where God has more for you, but you are afraid to let the past go? I've been there. I was there at this point in my life and now it was just me and God. What decisions would I make from here?

Sometimes God takes things away from us to show us how much we value that thing over God. We may not intentionally do it, but I was turning my family, friends, and relationships into little gods and placing them over God. It was time that I relinquished that status to reach my identity. I didn't know who I was, but who I was becoming was building a solid foundation in God. I was at the point where God was all I had. God began to slowly demolish everything that I put in front of Him so that He could become the forefront of my life. That was a hard concept for me to grasp and obedience was a big step.

PAIN. PROCESS. PURPOSE.

CHANEL CHASE

PAIN . PROCESS . PURPOSE .

YOUR INTIMATE THOUGHTS

Here's a section where I want you to reflect on the PAIN phase of your life. We all have encountered moments in our lives where we experienced pain. I pray that my story has begun to bless you and reveal some things in your life as well. Please feel free to share with yourself on these pages your own personal journey through pain.

Love Always,

Chanel

_____
_____
_____
_____
_____
_____
_____
_____
_____
_____
_____
_____
_____
_____
_____

PAIN. PROCESS. PURPOSE.

PAIN. PROCESS. PURPOSE.

PAIN. PROCESS. PURPOSE.

PART II: PROCESS
Chapter 5: Sex, Celibacy, and Obedience

When I say obedience was a big step, I probably should have said that it was a HUGE step. Putting away my own thoughts and allowing myself to be completely led by the Holy Spirit was a huge step into identifying who I am in Christ. There is a true process to getting through the pain in order to focus on you and become all God created you to be. After these events of relationships being ruined between me and my dad, friends, and my ex-boyfriend, God began to have me make some strong commitments to Him which I was unaware that I was ready to make. As I mentioned earlier, He was removing everyone and everything from my life so I would make Him the forefront. Sometimes, we don't realize the things that are holding us back from growth until God takes them away from us.

I was hiding from many things. I hid behind friends, family, materialistic things, "fake love," and so much more. Slowly but surely, God began to break down those barriers one by one. No longer did I put my relationship with my dad before God. I didn't put my friends before God, and I didn't have a dating relationship to put before God. Yet, God knew that my heart still yearned for love. I wanted true love, but earlier in the book we talked about first having to love yourself through the love of God. God asked me to do something that many people in their twenties aren't doing. One of the first things that God told me was that "I need you to be **CELIBATE.**" I remember the day I heard it, I laughed at God. **Are you serious? Celibacy?!?** How is that going to help the place I'm in? I didn't really understand what role this was going to play in my life, but I did hear from God very clearly and I knew that a new chapter of my life was getting ready to begin.

At the time, I truly had no idea why God would choose me to be celibate. Firstly, I wasn't having sex regularly. Secondly, I always tied sex to emotions, so I thought I had the right understanding of sex. Even though biblically, we are not supposed to have sex outside of marriage, it's the 20th century, and most people are. I had convinced myself that not being celibate was okay. I figured this would somehow tie back to my identity. Sex was another mask that was keeping me from finding my identity in God.

Love is something that every person yearns for. Who doesn't want to be loved? I mean, every person in this world longs for love from someone or something. As I began to build a closer relationship with God, I began to truly converse with Him about how this was going to help me. I had chosen to be obedient, but I still wanted to know how this related to my journey. I remember God telling me that I was just learning what love was, and then one night, God revealed something that stuck with me. He told me, *"I want you to experience love as I intended it to be between husband and wife."* Before, I related sex to love. If I had sex with someone, then of course, to me that meant they loved me. I was emotionally attached to the individuals I had sex with, and that in a way made them little gods in my head. I was so emotionally attached to my relationships that I didn't realize that sex played a major part in me thinking that I loved them because we were having sex. I needed to clear my mind of clutter. God was preparing me for my husband. It began the process of unmasking me to the core of who God designed me to be.

Sex was another mask. Sex was what I hid behind to justify that the man I was *"in lust with"* really loved me. I didn't understand love, and now I understood what God was trying to show me. However, my mind was still caught in the world, and I was trying to pull one foot out of the world to be grounded in the Word. In order to do that, I needed to listen to God, obey God, and know that God is love and has a plan in the end. It was a gradual process, one that would be a long journey to helping understand more and more about the masks that I was carrying on the inside. Think about it, how do you come to your closest friends and tell them about your new lifestyle change? Sometimes, doing what God tells us to do is the hardest part. In all honesty, if I would have been obedient in my friendships from the beginning, then God would have had the right people in my life. However, because I was disobedient, I had some that encouraged me on my journey and some that mocked the journey. That was my fault. For us to elevate in life, we must have some separation. I didn't separate when I was told by God, and that caused my journey to become harder than it needed to be. However, that was part of my process and necessary for my growth.

Preparing my mind for this process was going to be a challenge. This was just a part of my journey and it was a step toward obedience. Sometimes it truly takes some focus. I was in a place in my life where I was allowing my external factors to determine my internal movements. I allowed everyone around me to influence my thoughts without them even knowing that they were influencing me. I was worried about fitting in and people liking or disliking me. That was more important than what God had destined for me. That was my past. I was determined on taking the next step to where God wanted me to be. A lot of times when God is calling us to step out, we try to stay in. I was determined to come out of that layer of myself. I wanted a fresh start, but I truthfully didn't want to make that commitment to be different because I knew that the people that I was attached to would think I was crazy. Then, I began to realize that maybe those people were the very people that I needed to disconnect from to go to the next level.

At first, to be honest, not having sex wasn't even that difficult. The mask that it affected was the mask that allowed me to connect sex to love. I spent time by myself. If you've ever been by yourself then you would know that the process is bitter sweet. The time alone forced me to look at myself in the mirror. When I looked, I couldn't even see me. I just saw everything and everyone that defined me up until this point. Have you ever been there? I didn't know who I was and this process was allowing me to take ownership of that. I had been defined by what my parents told me I was, by what my friends thought I was, based on the car I drove, by what things I possessed, but deep down inside, the definition of me was missing. I let all that take so much of me, that I didn't recognize myself.

Remember earlier in the book, I told you that God explained to me that no one could ever love me until I first learned to love myself through the love of God. That was the key. How could I learn to love myself if I didn't know who I was? It took me lying on my back for a guy to define that he loved me and internally I didn't even love myself. I didn't have the value that was destined to be engraved in me, and I wasn't searching for it until now.

How many of you can relate to a time in your life where your value for yourself was not taken seriously? This is how I felt, but God opened my eyes by allowing me to protect the part of me that He created to be pure for my mate. It seemed like such a small part of the process of love and my identity, but it wasn't. It was the first step in learning how to love me. I chose to take back what was mine. I chose to regain who I was and live outside of the box of the world. I didn't want to just stop having sex, but I knew it was what God wanted me to do. At this point, I understood that there was a higher purpose to what God was doing in my life and somehow it was connected to my identity.

As I began to look in the mirror, I began to write on the mirror the things I felt about me. Some of the words were **scared, used, hurt, lost, ugly, ashamed, and so much more**. I couldn't see anything good. The respect I had for myself didn't go beyond what the guy that broke my heart felt. I was connected to his thoughts, his feelings, and I didn't know why. My respect for myself was connected to the things my dad said to me out of anger. As I looked in the mirror, I saw everything but happiness. I'm being raw and honest with you because we don't just experience pain and forget it. Pain will take us through a process, and it was the process that I was going through.

I remember spending many nights asking God why I couldn't just have my own thoughts, and why I felt like I was living through the thoughts of others. It was like a mystery until one night I had a dream. In this dream, it was me and Jesus. I began to cry as I ran towards Jesus, but throughout my path, I was being yanked apart and pulled astray. Memories of my past continued to pull me from the light I saw Jesus in. It was as if I was a puzzle and my pieces began to leave. The first piece left when I was a teenager and my dad and I argued day after day. The second piece left on the day I lost my virginity to a guy that God did not ordain for me. The third piece disappeared the day I decided to "fall in lust" with a stranger. The fourth piece went to the guy I thought that I was going to marry because he looked good on the outside. From that relationship, many pieces came off. They were pieces of my heart that I left for him to trample over. They coincided with the nights I was alone crying when I lost my dignity, or the night I allowed him to compare me to different women, or the night that I saw him in the club talking to another girl and turned my cheek because of embarrassment. They coincided with the nights I laid and had sex in fear of not being loved. Those were the pieces that were disintegrating my body as I tried to walk closer to God. Then, came the pieces of the puzzle from the decisions I made after we broke up. The many nights I cried, the many nights I got drunk and woke up not knowing where I was. The many nights I tried to fit in with the crowd but didn't belong. The decision I made to argue with my dad and not let go. Some pieces came from friendships that were broken because of my mistakes. All those decisions, all those circumstances; they all consumed me. Those were the pieces of the puzzle that were trying to hold me back. I remember trying to get closer and closer to the light, and by the time I got there, there was nothing but that one puzzle piece left. **Only one.** I was literally nothing. There was nothing left because I had given it all away. Those are the things that I thought defined me.

When I approached God, I asked him why there was only one piece left of me, and then I began to understand. He explained to me that this was the one piece of me that was supposed to birth who I was supposed to be. It was the innocence of my heart that was connected to His pure love. It had never left me; it was just buried under the junk I allowed to take precedence over God's love. When the pieces fell off, all the weight connected to them did as well. I was afraid to be different based upon who they assumed me to be. I was afraid to let go because I had infused their definitions as a part of me. I let God's love be buried deep inside of me.

That dream showed me my process. That dream showed me that there was a process for me, and that even though I made mistakes, I could turn my life around. It wouldn't be easy, but I knew in the end it would be worth it. Celibacy was playing a major role in my life because it was a step towards me trusting God and internally becoming pure again. I needed to become pure in my body, spirit, and thoughts. I was vowing to God to never let anyone control my thoughts, mind, body, or spirit ever again. I had chosen to marry God until He chose to give me my Boaz, and my Boaz would deserve the best version of me. I was making a conscious decision to become spiritually endowed with God, and to unveil a layer of my masks. It was a decision to look in the mirror and know that I was a child of God. That was a big step.

PAIN. PROCESS. PURPOSE.

CHANEL CHASE

PAIN.PROCESS.PURPOSE.

CHANEL CHASE

Chapter 6: Road to Finding My Identity

My lost identity was on a new journey of discovery, and I promised to only be intimate with God until He gave me the man who would be my husband. My journey helped birth the place in my life where I could feel tremendously lighter. This journey was the beginning of a huge process that was birthed from my pain. This journey is what I call the turning point in my life. I made a conscious decision to start walking in obedience and I removed a layer of my mask. I was no longer hiding behind me. I began to look myself directly in the mirror. This is where you must be honest with God. The moment when He makes things clear is when we must make a choice. We must choose a new path with God or another wandering path. This time, I wanted to make a new path with God and celibacy was a very defining moment in finding my identity.

I made that decision. I finally understood it. Not that I needed to understand it because I had to learn how to obey without understanding, but God eventually revealed to me a deeper meaning, and I knew that I was on the right path. We all know that when things are going good, of course, there is going to be something that comes with dealing with temptation, and unfortunately, there were to be many temptations that I would face. The fact that I decided to wait on God pushed my spiritual love towards God, but my flesh still wanted to be touched by someone. I still yearned to have earthly love because everyone around me was meeting their match. At that time, I had been single for two years.

When I first made the decision, I started over. I was focused. I was going to church every Sunday and even on Wednesdays. I made God's Word my companion. I didn't really go out. I began to shut myself off from the world. Seems like drastic behavior, right? Yes, it was, but I knew at that time in my life, it called for drastic measures. During this time, my dad and I were still not talking, my friends were withering away, and I truly was asking God for guidance. I felt stuck. I knew where I wanted to go with God. I knew what I needed to separate from, but at the same time, I didn't feel like I was going anywhere. God hadn't given me my husband. I thought that when I made the decision to be celibate, God was going to turn my life around and suddenly, I would meet the man of my dreams, but it didn't happen. My life remained in limbo. I was trying to do right, but then I started to feel myself moving backwards instead of forward. I stopped going to church as often. I stopped reading my bible as often, and all the desires of what everyone else around me was doing started to seep in. I remember asking God if I was making the right decision. It didn't feel right. Maybe I heard wrong. I questioned myself and tried to rationalize with exactly what God had already told me. I thought a miracle was going to happen, but this was a slow, steady, process. This process was going to take time, and there were multiple pieces to the puzzle that were going to have to be put back together.

After about a year of celibacy, I noticed that when I looked in the mirror, I saw a girl that didn't care to be loved. Instead, I wanted lust. I wanted the guys to look at me and want me the same way they wanted the other girls. This is how the devil works. He saw something good that God was getting ready to do, and he sent mental distractions. Has that ever happened to anyone else? I wanted to stay focused on God's purpose, but I couldn't. I felt like I needed to quit obeying God. I felt as if I was doing all these things differently, but nothing was happening. I wanted more than what God was giving me. I wanted to see results, and when I didn't, I felt the process wasn't working. I would look back at my old relationship and see how happy he was, and I didn't understand why I couldn't be like them. I wanted what everybody else was doing. I wanted it, and then I realized that I was linking lust back to my want for love, my want to fit in, and my desire to be a part of the crowd. But that wasn't the journey. I remember pleading with God, and I told him that I really wanted to quit. I told him that I really wanted to start having sex again. I wanted to fit in with everyone else. It looked fun. I had forgotten the fun. I wanted the emotional connection. I wanted to feel desired by someone again. I didn't understand how being celibate was helping. I did what God wanted for some time now, and nothing was happening the way **I imagined.**

When I uttered those words, I remember falling on my knees and having a heart to heart with God. This wasn't a bargain. I didn't get to just decide when God's plan was over. It was my job to push through what God wanted me to do despite my flesh. I was learning a great lesson. How many of us have really tried to bargain with God to get the results that we wanted? I wanted new results, but I didn't want the results in God's time, I wanted them in *my* time. I wanted God to move when I wanted Him to move. If He didn't, I assumed I wasn't in His will.

Through this process, I've learned that patience is something that we develop. Patience is a huge part of the journey. Patience allows us to keep moving towards a goal even if it takes time. I started thinking about the story of the guy and the bamboo tree. There were two men, and they both planted seeds, one man planted the seeds and failed to water it every day because he didn't see any results. The other man planted the seeds and watered and cultivated the seeds everyday even when he saw no results. Five years later, the one who remained consistent and patient, had a beautiful bamboo tree, but for five years everyone laughed and made fun of him for continuing to do something that didn't make sense. Now, I'm sure that guy had a friend that encouraged him, but from the outside looking in, there was nothing there. However, over time, there was something beautiful that happened. We must learn to be patient even when it doesn't make sense because our patience is created through part of the process. Patience produces trust, and trust is needed to get to the process of experiencing the true love of God even after pain.

The process to discovering our spiritual identities is never easy. We all have a process. I'm just telling mine. Feeling worthless and trying to experience love is what led me here. Was I willing to jeopardize my growth because I didn't feel like God was moving fast enough? Yes. Maybe I sound crazy, but a part of me truly wanted to stop listening to God because my patience was wearing thin. I wanted what everyone else had. I wanted love. I wanted God. I wanted sex. I wanted it all. But it wasn't my time.

PAIN. PROCESS. PURPOSE.

I was comparing other people's lives to mine. Have you ever done that? Have you tried to match yourself to the people around you to see where you stand? I have. That was what I was doing, and I needed God through this. I needed God even when I felt like His plan was failing. My identity depended upon the decisions that I made. It all connected. Decisions that we make can lead us down new paths that God didn't intend for us, and I was trying to find myself in the midst of being who I thought God wanted me to be. I had an end goal, but I was comparing myself to people who didn't have the same goals as me. I was measuring my progress based on their lives instead of looking to God. I was still lost. But this was part of the process. The journey to finding yourself in God isn't straight and narrow. It has curves, bumps, happiness, sadness, and everything else, but the difference between the past and now is that I recognized the decisions that had to be made.

My journey was beyond the surface of having sex or not having sex. The journey was about trusting God or not trusting God. It was hard. I dated, and would go on three to four dates and then guys would feel that it was time for us to have sex. I became uncomfortable. I was ashamed to tell them what God was doing in my life. I was afraid of my truth, but that is because they were not who God ordained for me. It is important that even in something as simple as a date that we learn to listen to God. I had to get to the point that the person who God would bring in my life would understand the process. I had to convince myself to be patient. I had to convince myself that trusting God was more important than these dates. But it wasn't easy. It was a part of the process. This was my life, and I had to learn how to look myself in the mirror and be happy with whom God was creating inside of me. That wasn't easy. It wasn't easy to be in limbo. It wasn't easy to look myself in the mirror and tell myself that God had something greater for me when it seemed like life was happening for everyone except me. I had to learn that it wasn't my season. It wasn't my time. I wasn't ready yet, but I was on the right path.

The process was for me to learn how to be with God, and only God. I had to learn to give God my attention in every area of my life and it started with the part that hurt me the most. It started with me learning that love didn't depend on an earthly companion, sexual relations, or attention. The love that I needed was the love that allowed me to be intimate with God. That was one step but it was just the beginning of the process.

The process went beyond the action of me being celibate; it was about the obedience and tests that would lead up to my testimony. I was at a place where I knew I needed to be better. I was at a place where it hurt, but I knew there was something great on the other side. For the mothers reading this book, when you first became pregnant, there was joy. Then, there was the process of nine long months of carrying the baby. There were probably some great nights and some bad nights. It was a process. Although you encountered the carrying for nine months, the result was a wonderful new addition to the family. I was in the "carrying pains" phase. I had to learn how to build myself up. I had to learn how to be separate from the world, and in tune with God. This was hard. It was a hard place for me because I had a double mind. I wanted to do right, but I also wanted the things that may have been wrong for me, but I kept going. I remained focused, and I didn't quit. I found a hunger for getting to where God wanted me to be and that ignited my spirit. I was focused, but not for long.

PAIN PROCESS PURPOSE:
THE 3 P'S TO FINDING YOUR SPIRITUAL IDENTITY

CHANEL CHASE

Chapter 7: Bumpy Roads

The devil had it out for me, and this time, he was determined to hit me where it hurt. I had just gotten to a point where I was content with my friends, my life, and my journey. I had peace that everything would be okay. Have you been there? Just at peace. It feels good when you are truly there, and you have given everything to God. I remember that. I remember being there, and I remember in a split moment, it began to wither away. I received one phone call that began to put me back into a painful place. It was a distraction, but it was one that cut deep. My dad was getting extremely ill, and we still were not talking. He still couldn't fathom looking at me. I would call, and would get no answer. I would reach out, and there would be no contact. At this point in my life, we hadn't talked for almost five months, and I was learning to adapt to the situation. Even though I reached out many times during the last five months, there were no answered calls, no texts back, and if I showed up to the house, he wouldn't even look at me. It was bad, but I knew my disobedience sparked it, and I was coping with the relationship. I was coming to terms with the fact that he would come around, but another visit to the hospital turned my world upside down. I knew my dad was sick. My dad had been going through a healing process for a very long time, but he was a true fighter. He fought harder than anyone I knew. When I was twenty, he had seven heart attacks in the month of January; it wasn't his time. When I was twenty-one, it got worse. By the time I turned twenty-two, his hospital visits had doubled, and by this time, it had gotten worse. I knew he was a fighter, but for the past five months, we hadn't talked and knowing he was in the hospital and I couldn't speak to him broke my heart. I couldn't even remember our argument, but I did remember that our relationship was ruined and it was very difficult to even acknowledge why.

I prayed about it. I talked to my mom about it. I talked to my friends about it. But nothing could calm my heart. I needed to see him. He was in the hospital, and he was getting worse, and I didn't know what to do. So, I made the decision to go see him in the hospital. I couldn't wait any longer, and I thought it was the right thing to do. I remember that day like it was yesterday. It was one of the worst days of my life. I remember walking in the room with tears in my eyes and telling my dad in person that I had to come see him. I remember looking at him in the hospital bed and asking him if we could talk. I reached out for a hug, and he just looked at me. He had no reaction at all. It was as if I wasn't there. I didn't exist. I told him that whatever we had going on was not worth my relationship with him. I told him that I loved him. Nothing at all. Just blank stares. When the nurse came in, she asked him who I was. He didn't acknowledge it. That hurt. But then, he asked me to leave, and that broke my heart. With tears in my eyes, I asked my dad if we could talk, and if I could just sit with him. He asked me to leave again. I know it was just the devil, but it hurt. It really hurt. The next time he asked me to leave and I didn't, he called security to escort me out. This is my dad who loved me my whole life but, because of one argument had security escort me from his hospital room. I couldn't believe it. I was devastated. It hurt, and I didn't know why it had gotten to this horrible point.

I remember the whole drive home, I cried. I asked God what would happen if he left this earth and we never spoke again. How was anything in my life ever going to be fixed? It didn't make sense. I needed my dad. I always had my parents, but at this moment, I was at my lowest point. How could I look myself in the mirror knowing that one of the people who made me couldn't even look at me? I was escorted out of a hospital for visiting my dad. I couldn't make any logic out of any of this. My heart was broken, and I didn't know what to do. I was mad at God. I was mad at myself, and I was mad at my dad. But there wasn't anything I could do. This was one of the hardest lessons that I would learn, and I had to go through it. It was part of the process.

After that trip to the hospital, I spent many days worrying. I spent many days frustrated. I spent many days reaching out to my dad, and nothing was working. I didn't want us to be on bad terms, and I didn't understand why God would allow this to continue knowing that I was trying to stay on the right path. Why did He allow our relationship to go through this? What was the benefit? I didn't understand. I didn't understand what this situation had to do with my journey, but at the time I didn't care. I wanted what I wanted. I wanted my dad to talk to me. I wanted our relationship to go back to normal. I wanted what felt like punishment to go away. I wanted this situation to be over.

The problem with everything that I was thinking was that it all centered on what "I wanted." Not once during this process did I ever think about what was going on with my dad. The story in my mind was told from my perspective. It was told from my heart. I didn't think about what God was doing in my dad's life. For a month after that situation, I pushed God away. I didn't pray. I didn't read my Bible. I didn't go to church. My feelings toward myself were not pleasant. I'd try to laugh with my friends, but inside I felt defined by not being worthy enough to even be in the presence of my dad. It was rough. I acted out. I began to drink excessively again. I was having a relapse. It was bad, but something in me still held on to the one thing I made a vow to be obedient to….celibacy. I held onto the obedience through all the other things I was going through. It was weird, but it was my one piece of promise that I could uphold. It was the only area where I felt that I was getting things right. I was testing God through this, but I didn't realize that the test was on me. It wasn't about the act that I was doing. It was certainly about my trust and obedience to God. It was my vow, and it was hopefully something that could turn my thinking around.

One night, I was really intoxicated at my house. I woke up and walked to my mirror. I looked horrible. My hair was messed up. My eyes were red and puffy. It looked as if I had been crying all night. I looked and asked myself, "Did I feel better?" The truth was, I didn't. I was tired of hiding behind what was easy. I was afraid to face the difficult truth. I wasn't ready to face myself. As I stood there, I realized that I had fallen back into the web of people. I had let Satan win. I allowed an earthly person, my dad, to dictate how I felt about myself. At this moment, I realized that he was human. None of us are perfect. My dad wasn't perfect. I wasn't perfect, and we all made mistakes. My relapse wasn't helping me. I needed to get back on track. It was time for me to be who God wanted to me. I had to learn to trust God even through the bad. I had to see the storm, and realize that there was a better outcome. Have you ever been disgusted with the decisions you made due to frustration or anger? Have you ever had a relapse in your relationship with God? This is where I was. I was realizing that nothing I was currently doing was helping the situation that I was facing. I was drowning in my own sorrows. I was making my situation worse. It wasn't healthy. At this point, I was angry that I ruined my progress, even though I had one area where I remained obedient.

Sometimes as we go through these trials of life, there are things that we hold onto that have made a significant impact in our lives. For me, the decision I made with God to be celibate was my reminder of my journey. That was the one thing that I could hold onto and remind myself of what God brought me through. It gave me hope. It was the one thing that reminded me that God could remake me as a person. That was my symbol of obedience. Have you had a similar, significant moment in your life? I had to learn that God was in control, and I needed to learn to trust Him. It was time for me to stop faking it. It was time for me to move forward. My dad was sick. He wasn't talking to me. It was hurtful, but it was my story. No one on this earth could change it. Only God.

Remember when I referred to the process of carrying a baby for nine months. This was my carrying stage. These were the situations that I was carrying in my heart. These were the trials I had to work out during my carrying stage. When a woman is pregnant, they don't see the baby growing every day. At points in the pregnancy, they can get ultrasounds and see what is going on with the baby, and the doctor has different appointments to check on the growth of the baby. That is how I had to look at this stage. I was at a point where I was carrying my situations. During the process, I may have had some setbacks, but there were appointments that I needed self-checkups with God. I needed God to tell me that through my struggles, it was going to be okay. I was going to produce a healthy and powerful purpose, and I was going to be fine despite the circumstances. My spiritual father needed to check my heartbeat and make sure that it was still breathing for him. He needed to show me that He would help me go through that carrying stage, and just like that mother that is pregnant goes to classes to prepare for the birth, He was going to be with me to prepare for the birthing of the new me.

It was all the process. Sometimes, it's hard to give things to God, but it's a vital part of the journey to finding who you are in God. *Cast your cares upon the Lord for he cares for you* (1 **Peter** 5:7 **KJV**) had to become my anthem. It had to become something I truly believed. During this process, I had to learn that the situations that happen beyond my control had to be given to God. There was no way around it. I wanted to give up. I wanted to stop. I wanted to just give up on me because I felt my dad gave up on me. There was a still small voice that was in the back of my head telling me that there was a plan. I didn't understand the plan, but there was a plan.

We must learn to listen when God tells us that there is a plan. I didn't know what it was, but I had to learn to move without thinking about anything other than what God told me. I had to learn how to depend on God. When everyone else left me, God never did. I had to remember that through the months and months that passed from that point on that my dad didn't talk to me. I had to remember that each time that I longed for love from an earthly person and didn't receive it. I had to learn that it's not my timing, but God's timing that matters. My season involved these trials and tribulations that would help shape me, but they wouldn't define me. I had to stop having a pity party about life and get to a place where God was my joy. It didn't depend on any outside factors. I was going through the trials and tribulations of life, but I was beginning to step into a higher purpose. That lead me to my period of separation, and that's where I began to push towards a new dimension of myself in Christ.

PAIN
PROCESS
PURPOSE:
THE 3 P'S TO FINDING YOUR SPIRITUAL IDENTITY

Chapter 8: Spending Time Alone with God

Separation leads to elevation. I had to keep telling myself that every time I thought anything negative about my process. I had truly begun to separate from *everything*. I came to peace with the situation with my dad, and I was learning how to love myself. I was even distant from my close friends. They hadn't done anything wrong. It was just a necessary part of the process. I was finally at the point where it was just me and God. I prayed instead of listening to music. I wrote journals to God instead of watching television, and I went to church instead of going out. I was on a hiatus towards self-development in God, and it felt real. The process of all the trials and tribulations was coming to an end, and I was truly learning how to focus on God. I was learning to listen to His voice and for His voice. Separation did that. I still didn't fully know how to be alone, but I was learning.

Has life ever taken everything from you and forced you to rebuild? That's where I was. Life had taken every ounce of emotion from me, and I was building it up again, except this time, I was building it with God. This was vital in my journey to my spiritual identity. I was learning how to rely on God alone. It was a good thing. I was learning that I couldn't put people in front of God's vision for my life. I was learning that only God could fill my voids. We have all looked for other people's approvals, but a major part in learning during my journey was being 1000% happy with me. I learned how to have uninterrupted time with God, and in that time, I had many self-evaluations about the person that I was.

PAIN. PROCESS. PURPOSE.

How many times have you planned to spend time with God and your best friend calls or something comes up that distracts you? This is quite common. We may talk about God, but we must also spend time with God. We treat him as if He is a check on the to-do list, but we never embrace Him as a person. We treat Him as an option that we get to when we have done everything else that is important to us. During my time of separation, learning to embrace my relationship with God was paramount. I needed to embrace God as a person and get to know Him as my friend. A lot of us talk about Jesus because we have seen what He has done in our lives, and honestly, most of that is done by default. He watches over us because He loves us. However, knowing God is a different ball game. I remember when that revelation became clear to me. I knew "of God" my entire life. I knew that He was awesome. I relate this to thinking about our favorite reality star. We love them because of their appearance on television. I loved God because of his appearance in the church, but I didn't know Him. I knew of Him. How many of us really know God? In pondering over this question, I thought about how many people really knew me? People knew I had a fancy job, a car, a house, and whatever else they heard about me, but they didn't know the pain or frustration I was going through. They didn't talk to me. They saw me. That was how I viewed God. I knew what He could do in my life based upon what others told me He had done in their lives. I heard how He saved this person. I saw Him working in my parents' lives, but I didn't know God until I embraced him.

My spiritual identity was tied to God, but I didn't know Him personally. I didn't know myself, and I needed to know God to build myself up to a confident place. I didn't even know how to start that process, but I did know that it was necessary. My separation allowed me to put my focus on God, and I began with a small journal called my "Thank You God" journal. I used to begin with just thanking God for the small things He did though I didn't deserve it. Not that we can ever do anything to earn our love from God, but I would just thank Him for keeping me when I felt unworthy. I would thank Him that I woke up and I was healthy. It was simple, but one thing this new place of thankfulness ignited was a fire to show me how much God had truly done in my life. It was overwhelming. From that, I began to cry out and sob and sing and dance. It became about being intimate with God. I began to share my deepest thoughts in my journal. My prayers turned into conversations. I had a struggle with reading the Bible; it was hard for me. I didn't understand it, but I started listening to God tell me what to read. It was not that easy in the beginning, but my journey to get there helped me understand first hand God's unconditional love for me. My separation created the time for God to expose me to the small things I'd overlooked. It was about listening. If we can't listen to the voice of God within us, then we will never embrace the relationship.

Let me explain. If you are dating a person and they never call you, but they say they love you, would you believe them? Or if you were dating a person and you never go on a date, would you believe that spending time with you was a priority to them? I would hope the answer would be no to both of those questions because it's obvious. However, if we put that same scenario on God, then we would create a bunch of excuses. God wants us to treat Him like any friendship or relationship. It requires a cultivating of the seeds in the relationship. We must spend time with God. We must make Him a priority. We must put Him above everything else in our lives. This was a learning process for me. I needed this time of separation.

I'm a firm believer in spiritual gifts, and I truly wanted my journey to mean something. I wanted to get to the purpose that God intended for me. I wanted to listen. I wanted to be obedient. I wanted to stay on the right path. I wanted to use my gifts for good. I didn't want to be run by people's emotions. I didn't want outside influence. I wanted to spend more private time with God so that He could show me a deeper meaning for my existence beyond just being here. This was part of my journey. All of this would soon play a part in defining who I was, and what my spiritual identity was. If I continued to hide behind the many masks I had worn my entire life, I would never experience the things God had for me. Sometimes it takes us having faith to move outside of our comfort zones into where God has designed for us to be. No one's journey is the same, but I know when we embrace God, we will find our spiritual identity.

This process of pain taught me so much. This is a process that can't be rushed. I couldn't tell God how I wanted to get here. I couldn't tell God when I wanted to get here, but without the trials of the process, it wouldn't mean as much to me. Many people like to look at their past and compare it to others' stories, but the truth is, everyone has a different destiny. We get so caught up in this world of comparison that we don't recognize what God is doing in our lives. During this time of separation, I didn't just embrace God, I also embraced myself.

Did you know that our attitudes can affect our altitudes? It can affect how far we go in life. So many of us want to reach a height of success, but we spend more time taking a pessimistic approach to thinking rather than an optimistic approach. An optimistic person by definition is a person who is hopeful and confident about the future. Therefore, a pessimistic person would be the opposite. This was me. I was a pessimistic person and in my journey, I had to embrace and recognize my weaknesses before I could correct them. How would you categorize yourself in this situation? Separation taught me that misery loved company. If I consistently had a pessimistic approach to thinking then it was very likely that the people I associated with regularly thought that way also. It took me stepping out of the world and going into a personal cocoon to get to a point to recognize that my circle didn't reflect where God had intended me to go. The more I embraced my relationship with God, the more He embraced His plan for unveiling my spiritual identity. He began to show me more about my future and the direction I was going. I was previously concerned when God didn't move as fast as I wanted Him to. I hadn't elevated to the level where God needed me to be to push me to my next level.

It was me. I had a pessimistic attitude. I was always thinking the worse.

I was always frustrated. I was unhappy. I was lost. I wasn't ready. In (1 Thessalonians 5:16-18 NIV), the Bible states, *"Rejoice always, pray without ceasing, give thanks in all circumstances; for this is the will of God in Christ Jesus for you."* If we are supposed to rejoice always, where does that leave room to form negative thoughts? I only liked to embrace God when it was convenient for me, and any other time, I would think very negatively about myself and what God had for me. The truth is, we all have been there, but we should learn to be uplifting no matter the circumstance. Our journey could be what God is using to bless someone. I never thought about it like that. I never thought that my positive attitude could be grace or happiness to the people around me. I began to think back to my relationship with my dad and my ex and all the people I encountered, and I realized that I could have made a difference. I could have been a better person in every circumstance, but I chose not to be.

These were all self-reflections. I separated from people to grow as a person. That was a part of my spiritual journey. I was a pessimistic person. I blamed everyone around me without looking at myself. God helped me through that, and He can help anyone through that thought process. I didn't realize that God is truly testing us when things are not going well in our lives. I used to look at my relationships and the trials that surrounded them as punishment, but I dug a little deeper to see them as God preparing me for the future. During this time, I began to rejoice about the things that I had overcome. I knew whatever it was, God was going to use it to seriously bless me later. My trust grew with God. My faith grew with God. This separation was the key to finding myself through God. I was on the path to a spiritual identity birthing, and these trials and tribulations were the pregnancy. I was going through my tests, and although I made mistakes, God was still with me.

I remember one night I had a serious talk with God and He asked me a question that truly puzzled me, "Do you uplift or destroy?" My first instinct was, of course, to say that I uplift people. Then, I began to take a closer look at the small details of my life. I complained so much. I was frustrated. I was mad at God. I blamed people and never took responsibility. Was I really operating in the love of God with a heart to bring people closer to Him? No, I wasn't. I was operating in the world. He asked me, "What was I spreading?" I remember laughing because I didn't quite get it, but then He told me that every time I open my mouth, I spread good or bad. I work for Him or the devil. Then, I understood. My life had not been about the purpose that God intended it to be. My life was about me and when I spoke, my words held no value for God. I was broken without Him, and I was coming to an understanding of how much I played a role in everything and every decision I made in my life. Thinking positively and being optimistic go hand in hand with faith and trusting God. We need faith to believe what we can't see and to be positive about the future. We have to have faith in our visions. I didn't represent that. I would spread negativity. It was like a disease. It spread to every person I came in contact with, and during my phase in life, there were some people that I pushed away. It wasn't everyone else's fault. God began to show me myself in the light. I was beginning to see clearer, and my journey to God was becoming more evident. It wasn't people I needed. It wasn't validation I needed. I was validated by God. All I needed was God connected to my provision, and I was on the road to execution. God knew what was intended for my spiritual identity to birth, but it was up to me to push myself with God into the next dimension. How many of us need to be pushed? We must stop letting our past define who and whose we are. There are only two sides. If we are not working for God, then we are working for the devil. That revelation changed my life. The minute I began to put my focus on God and truly embrace a relationship with Him, my life changed. I began to accelerate into my purpose and my spiritual identity was growing.

PAIN . PROCESS . PURPOSE .

Your Intimate Thoughts

Here's a section where I want you to focus on the **PROCESS** phase of your life. As much as pain played a role in your life, it also birthed a process that you have gone through. I pray that you all take the time to journal about your process, and try to find God in your situation. Try to be as honest with yourself as possible because that will allow you to recognize how much God has helped you along the way.

Love Always,

Chanel

Pain. Process. Purpose.

PAIN . PROCESS . PURPOSE .

PAIN. PROCESS. PURPOSE.

PART III: PURPOSE
Chapter 9: Leading To My Purpose

After all the pain that I endured over the years, I was finally in my happy place. It was a place where I felt that God had blessed me with *"that peace that surpasses all understanding (Philippians 4:7 ESV)."* This was my turning point towards my purpose, and I was leaning towards God for my direction. I felt like a new Christian. Have you ever been around someone who just accepted Christ into their lives? Those people are on fire for Jesus every day. That's how I felt. I felt a radiating light shining through my body that represented the joy that I saw in Jesus every day. I prayed consistently. I read my Bible consistently. I felt as if no one could deter me from God. I was in a place where God was with me and I knew it. For the first time in a long time, I felt as if my pain led me to peace. My life was turning around, and the best part was that I was confident in who and whose I was. It was the beginning to something great. Nothing had changed externally. My life was still spinning. My dad and I still were not speaking. I had many friends who were no longer friends. I was still sort of isolated, but the difference was that God had begun to fill every single void that I felt. That's the best part of getting to a place of peace. The devil cannot touch what God is going to do. The devil can try to distract you in your journey, which he did with me, but he could not take away what God demanded for my life. I decided to walk in the shoes God had already ordained for me. My situation had not changed, but my internal thought process had certainly changed. I had begun to move from being a spiritual baby to a child, and although it seemed like a small stepping stone, internally I felt the change.

The turning point of your situation allows God to connect with you where you are. Sometimes God allows us to go through situations to prepare us for what is to come. When I began to think about it, I thought about my journey of learning how to ride a bike. My dad put the training wheels on my bike, and I thought that I was the bomb.com. I could whip around in that bike, but I was using a crutch. I was leaning on something to keep me grounded, my training wheels. I remember the day that my dad told me that it was time to take the training wheels off and I cried. I cried, and I cried some more. The first time on the bike, I tried to move by myself, but I couldn't. I fell. I would scream to my dad to just hold on to me. I wanted to use him to keep me afloat because I didn't know how to balance on my own. I was scared for him to let me go because when he did, I knew I was going to fall. But one day after many days of scraped knees and elbows, I rode my bike without the training wheels. I learned how to ride despite the many times I fell. Everything my dad told me finally clicked. It was just me, the bike, and the wind, and the lessons that my dad taught me helped me learn how to ride without the training wheels.

That is how our relationships with God are. We get to a point to where we feel like we are the bomb.com. We lean on the support of us, and we think that we are doing everything by ourselves. That is how it was with my training wheels. I felt like I knew how to ride the bike because I could whip it around everywhere with the training wheels on. However, there was an invisible support that was holding me afloat even when I didn't have balance in my life. When the training wheels were taken off, I realized how I was not doing it alone. I screamed for my dad. That is how we are in our relationships with God. We take off on our own paths and don't realize that God was taking us down the path that would lead us to our purpose. However, when we get in a bind and have gone through every situation, we scream to God for help. Just like my dad leaned towards me to try to guide me, God does the same for us. Sure, I fell and had many scraped knees and elbows, but that is how we are with God. We go down our path and God has his hand on us, but the scraped knees and elbows are the representations of our trials and tribulations. We experience the pain, but it's a part of the process. After we go through that, we reach a place where the experiences have been engraved in our hearts with God and we can continue in life knowing that God is with us. That was where I was when I finally could ride without the training wheels.

PAIN. PROCESS. PURPOSE.

Our spiritual journeys are like the process of learning to ride a bike. After all that I had been through on this journey, I was finally at a place where it was just me, God, and my experiences that were allowing me to go forward with my purpose. I was in a place of peace. That didn't mean that I wouldn't fall again, but this time, if I did, I knew I could get back up with confidence that God would still lead my life. Have you ever gotten to this point? It's a place where you feel like your life is coming together. I was just waiting on God to tell me what was next and lead my every move. This journey taught me to just wait on God, and He would work it out. That is truly what began to take place. He began to work out situations from the back end. The relationship with my dad still was not going well, but I would pray. I stopped trying to fight with my dad. I stopped trying to reach out. I began to use my experience with God to put God's Word on the situation.

Many months, I had been beating myself up about the mistake I made with my dad. I kept blaming myself. I was still hurt, but I was trying to trust God. I would pray many nights. I would cry. I would write, but God was removing pain day by day. It was the day after my twenty-fifth birthday that God allowed a shift to take place. It was a journey, but God did it. The day after my birthday, my mom was meeting me to give me my birthday card. I had no idea that my dad was with her. As my mom approached me, my dad didn't speak. He didn't say anything. He just looked at me, gave me a card, hugged me and during the hug, many burdens and yokes were being destroyed. I had been going through that situation for almost a year, and a day after my birthday, my dad and I were on the road to recovery. This is how God works. He began to turn my life around when I allowed Him to take control. Our relationship was not perfect, but there was a restoration. God restored something that was missing in my life. He restored a relationship that had been broken, but during that, He prepared me to receive the relationship that would lead to something bigger.

A couple of months later, friendships that had been broken were being restored. God was moving in my life, but it was all for a greater purpose. God was surrounding me with the people that He knew would need to be connected to me for the purpose He created. I trusted God, and my life was turning around. God was revealing how my life was in His hands, and if I continued to trust Him, my life would begin to shift. I began to open my eyes and live my life with a unique perspective. I was happy. I didn't feel lost. I didn't feel useless. I didn't feel broken. I felt like everything was falling into place. Everything that had been broken was becoming whole. But more importantly, I had changed. I had gone through life without trusting God, but I now realized that God could change me from the inside out. God re-wrote my plan, and I was discovering my purpose. Everything was happening for a reason. God never allows things to happen by mistake, and I was realizing that everything I had gone through was preparing me for this moment in my process. We should never think that what we have gone through defines our end. God still has a plan for us and the dots will continue to connect.

Over the next couple of months, things were getting better and better. My dad and I were better than we had ever been. This was nothing but God. Our relationship grew. We were nourishing something that had been broken far beyond those nine months of no communication. We were creating something new. Our relationship wasn't perfect, but it was God led. We would text all the time and God had restored so much that had been broken. It was amazing. God had healed so much, and He deserved all the credit, but it was still a process. It was a process we were working through together. I needed my dad, and he needed me. The voids that were being filled were life changing. I had layers of hurt beginning to fall off. Life was great, well our relationship was great, but my dad's battle was beyond our relationship.

The devil was coming to attack everything that God had begun to restore. That's how the enemy works, and this was a true test of my spiritual journey. Our relationship was restored in August. We had many months of dinners, father/daughter dates, phone calls, and texts. We were on the road to a long relationship, but the devil had plans. Four months after our relationship was restored, all hell broke loose. Everything that could have gone wrong did. **Everything**. My dad and I were just getting to better than normal, and a doctor report comes in to say that my dad may only have six more months to live. My world shattered. I tried to pray. I tried to find my faith, but at this moment, nothing but fear began to take over my life. Right on the cusp of something so great, the devil was working very hard. The devil was trying to destroy our family. The devil was on a mission for my peace to be destroyed and for my dad's life to be destroyed. It was something so horrific. The thought of my dad not being on this earth truly just made my heart hurt, but I knew I had to pull it together. I knew that my tears were not helping the situation. I knew that frustration was not helping the situation. I knew that worrying was not helping the situation, but I was hurting. I knew that this was where the paradigm shift that had taken place needed to come into effect. I needed to dig very deep and find God even when it was extremely hard to see him. Have you ever gone through anything that pushed you to find God during a storm? This is how I felt. I was trying to find the light in the middle of what the devil wanted to be darkness. I remember that night, I cried and I prayed. I cried and I prayed. And I cried and I prayed some more. I knew what I had to do, but I wanted to be angry. I wanted to be upset, but I didn't allow the devil to do that. I knew that I had a brother who needed to see strength. I knew I had a mother who needed someone to lean on, and I knew I had a God that could perform miracles. It was hard, but it was a turning point in the direction, and I needed to choose what path I was going to take. This would be hard, but I would have to decide. When difficult times came, I was faced with the decision to trust God or play into the devil, and this time in my journey, I wanted to trust God.

This was all hard for me. That was my dad, but I also knew the relationship and trust that I was forming with God. I tried to make the best out of a situation. I looked to God for help. Whitney Houston said it best in her song, "I look to you." I literally had no more strength by myself, and I knew I needed to lean on God. This time I was focused on what God wanted me to do and not how my human nature wanted me to react. I remember it was a couple of weeks before Christmas when that news was given to us. I prayed to God about what to do, and I remember God telling myself to embrace the restoration. Basically, I couldn't worry about what was going on; I had to focus on what God was doing. Has anyone ever been in a situation where you wanted to focus on the problem instead of the progress? This was me. I was focusing on the problem that doctors stated, but I wasn't focused on the process that God was taking me through. My mind shifted at that very moment. I was going to try to make this Christmas awesome.

I remember reaching out to every friend and family member that I knew had something to say about my dad and asking them to record a short little video about what my dad had done in their lives. I started off also telling my dad what he had done in my life as well. I made a cute YouTube video and I bought him a tablet that played the video constantly in the hospital room. I was determined to make it the best Christmas ever. He was in the hospital, but I was determined to make the hospital home, but God did something even better. On Christmas Eve, my dad was released from the hospital and we spent Christmas at home as a family. We watched the video on the TV as a family, and I remember the joy it brought to my dad. I remember the tears that it produced. I remember that moment. God moved. I listened. This time I learned to obey God when He told me, and the process of obedience prevailed. I saw a light in my dad I hadn't seen in a while. I saw hope. The next day my dad was admitted back to the hospital, but that one day changed his perspective. I allowed God to give me an idea that allowed me to create a shift in my dad's mind. He spent Christmas home with his family, and watched a long video about how he has made an impact in so many people's lives. That was God.

PAIN
PROCESS
PURPOSE

THE 3 P'S TO FINDING YOUR SPIRITUAL IDENTITY

CHANEL CHASE

Chapter 10: Realizing God's Greater Purpose

This was where I began to see that God was going to use me more as I listened to Him. I was headed to my purpose. The lost time I spent trying to find myself was created for times like this. I found strength in God that kept me during this storm, and God was continuing to work in my life. It felt good to reap the benefits of obedience. It showed me how the process I went through was helping me to make better decisions in times of purpose. Think about where this time is in your life. Where was one of the first significant changes in your walk with God? It may be right now while reading this book, but God will use us all. We must just be willing to walk through the process to peak at our future. It was the beginning of a birthing of purpose, and it is important to remember that God still has a plan for our lives as we are going through our spiritual journeys.

The one thing about what was happening with my dad and I, was that I realized that God could take something dead and breathe life into it. It wasn't that I hadn't heard it before, but I experienced it. I saw a dead relationship be brought back to life, and it was only by the hands of God that I experienced that. We grow more in God when we experience God in our own lives. I was so used to hearing other people's stories, but I was watching my tests become testimonies, and that was life changing. I was experiencing God, and He was using me as a tool.

Through this journey, God began to talk to me. I learned how to have real conversations with God. I put away the cliché version of God and dug deeper. I was experiencing His love, I was experiencing His favor, I was experiencing being in the will of God, and I was experiencing God in my life. This is what it felt like to still have issues and skeletons in my past, but for God to see a future. The more I elevated spiritually, I began to see how God was miraculously working in my favor. God was placing me in the divine corner of people who were going to assist me to getting to my purpose. He was taking toxic relationships out of my life, and He was embedding life fulfilling relationships. I felt the change. Just as Jekalyn Carr wrote in her song "Greater is Coming." I literally felt the shaking in my life. I felt like God was moving in ways that I could not explain. I felt things internally shifting. I felt my life changing. I felt my spirit moving away from spirits that did not align with my purpose. I was learning God. I knew I needed the shifting in my life, and this process was preparing me for my purpose.

This is the story of the pain that leads to the process that produces the purpose. This explains what God was doing in my life and what He can do in yours. I was going through a supernatural change in a natural world, but I was allowing God to take control. I was on my spiritual journey, and I was working to walk into my spiritual identity. God was producing purpose. The relationships that I had were not going to take me to where God intended for me to be, but He was moving me into the place that would attract me to the people that needed to be a part of the journey. This took me being humble enough to serve the people God placed in my life to get to the crowd that God was connecting me to. He embedded friends that prayed. He embedded friends that would visit my dad in the hospital with me. He embedded the people that would build my faith when I wanted to give up. He began the process of preparing me for my purpose.

God will do that. God removed people I thought would be life-long friends, and replaced them with people that would stretch me. This did not happen until I had an open mind and trusted in God in every area of my life including my friends. How many of us have heard God tell us that our season was up with someone and we continued anyway? This is an area we must train our minds to trust God. He will *never leave us nor forsake us* (**Deuteronomy 31:6**). This was something I had to learn. I wasn't doing anything wrong, but when I prayed to God to reveal my spiritual identity and take me to my purpose, it involved removing people that have outstayed their season. We all must do that. We must go through our spiritual closet and see what we are still holding onto that needs to be given away. We must learn to let go. I was learning this. I was learning that my journey was not attached to the people that I was with. My journey was elevating, and God would put the people in my life that were going to pull me to the higher level where God intended for me to be. God was going to bless me with exactly what I needed, but before God could bless me, He had to prepare me. The process of getting to where God wants you to be starts with a process that may be painful, but it births things in you that allow you to level up. In lieu of what was coming, God knew that my circle would need to be strong, and that eventually everything would tie together.

As God began to change my friendships, He also began to change my past thoughts on relationships. He began to renew my mind from where I was, to where I was going. I allowed my pain to justify my view on relationships. Have you ever done that? Have you ever allowed the hurt of one relationship to hinder the one that would follow? I allowed that relationship to define who I was. However, God changed that. He showed me what love was, and then He created a promise of celibacy to show my obedience to Him. It was focused on my relationship with God, and He would soon show me what that was leading into.

Right after my tumultuous four-year relationship with my ex-boyfriend that stripped me of my identity, I created all these stipulations for God on the man I needed to come into my life next. Of course, he needed to love God, but in addition to that, I told God how handsome and tall I wanted him to be. I informed God that my man would not have any kids or prior situations. He would need to be smart, funny, have lots of money in the bank, and so much more. I created the perfect man. I wrote it down and made it plain. It was a list of 20 distinct characteristics describing my new guy. I wanted that. I prayed on that. I wanted God to make that happen for me. I was waiting for God to answer. Then, about 8 months later I asked God, why hadn't He given me the guy that I wanted? Why hadn't He given me the guy that I had been praying about? What was the issue? I recall it as if it was yesterday, God told me that **He didn't work by what I wanted, but He would show me what I needed.**

From that point on, in my head, I still knew what I wanted, and I just believed that my wants and needs would align in God's eyes. I thought that God was just making me exercise patience. A couple of months later, I met a guy, and he seemed cool. He said he loved God, he didn't have any kids, he was smart, nice, funny, well established, tall, and good looking. He seemed like the perfect match. I was taken on date after date, and it seemed to be getting kind of serious. Our conversations were good, not great, but good, and I felt like I needed to see how he would interact with my friends. So, we went on a couple double and triple dates and we had fun. It was just that, fun. It didn't get any deeper than that. I was forcing myself to try to make this work because I had been single for so long. I wanted this to be the guy from my checklist, but it didn't seem like it was going to work. So, I asked my friends. When I asked their opinion, it was bland, and they would say he's cool or seems nice, but never anything that was like, yes, he's the one for you. Remember when God elevated my circle? He gave me a group of friends that would help keep me focused, so that opinion wasn't the confirmation that I would need to keep seeing this guy.

That night, I had a heart to heart conversation with God and asked him what was going on. Then, God told me that he wasn't the guy that he had given me, and that I had moved without listening. I decided to take this guy off my checklist. This relationship had nothing to do with God. It wasn't in God's plan for me. Do we ever ask God if the person that we are dating is the one who He planned for us? I didn't in this situation. I thought he was everything that I wanted, except my heart didn't really like it. We didn't connect how I thought the man that God sent to me would. He just fit the check boxes on my list, but I thought God fulfilled my prayers. It wasn't God, it was the enemy. This man was a distraction, and I fell into the trap. I fell into the trap of what I wanted versus what God wanted. Sometimes, the devil gives us things that look like they are from God, but unless we hear confirmation from God, it is not from Him. *The thief comes to steal, kill, and destroy* **(John 10:10 NIV)**, and that is what he was trying to do with me. When Satan saw something good that God had planned in my future, he tried to send another distraction. That is why during our spiritual journey, it is imperative that we learn to trust God in all areas, even dating.

This was a learning experience. It was something I had to go through. I was truly wasting this guy's time because I knew that he wasn't the one that God intended for me to be with. He was meant for someone else. Satan was deterring both of us from where we were intended to go. This guy was just something the devil put in front of me to distract me from the plan God wanted for me. Previously I was distracted, and I didn't want to go back down that road. I chose my last path, and this time, I wanted God to choose! Have you ever made the mistake of dating the wrong person? Have you let your desires deter you from God's plan? I did, and when I realized that is what I had done, I decided that God had to be the one to give me the person that *He* had prepared for me. I couldn't write my own story. God designed a person for me, and I decided to wait on God. I didn't want to *pretend* to wait on God, but I wanted to wait on God. I stopped praying for the things on my list, and

I would pray that God would send me the person that He designed for me. I prayed that whoever it was would be sent by God. This was a shift in my dating life. I encourage everyone reading this book to pray for the one God has for you. We can be deceived by many, but God will direct our paths to tell us yay or nay. I was just patient. I waited. And waited. And waited.

PAIN.PROCESS.PURPOSE.

CHANEL CHASE

Chapter 11: God Has a Plan

During this time of waiting, I was still dealing with the struggles of my dad being in and out of the hospital. Everything was going bad, but I was still trying to remain positive. I didn't want the devil to win in the situation, and it was hard. There were a lot of tests in this period of waiting, where God allowed me to grow. He was preparing me for what was to come. When God begins to show us our purpose, He begins to use the people around us to reveal certain messages. It was my time to be used. My dad's self-esteem was very low now. He had always been the provider during every situation. He was the one who had taken care of our family for our entire lives, but he was ashamed of where he was. My mother was out working, and the roles were reversed. My dad was down, and this was hard for him. It was a change for our family, and a change for him. He wanted to be the loud, joyous, and helpful person that he was on the inside, but his body was not cooperating. It was difficult, but we got through it. My dad had to learn that we were his family, and we would have his back regardless of the situation. The beauty in this happening is that God allowed our relationship to strengthen even more than it was. God was growing our bond. We used to never sit and talk, and now we were. We could have serious conversations. Going through this with my dad was changing me. My heart was opening, and I felt the warmth of bonds being mended.

I recall one day at the hospital when my dad was very discouraged. My mom wasn't there. My brother wasn't there. It was just me. There were a couple of arguments that had taken place, and everyone needed a break. My dad was so flustered and upset, and I talked to him about all the changes in his life. I asked him how he felt. He was down. He lost his mother in January of that year, and his breathing was not intact. He felt the control of his manhood was diminishing. On top of that, the doctors were telling him that he was going to lose his life. Everything was going wrong, and we sat there and talked. I told him that it reminded me of the story of Job. *Job was the wealthiest man in a land known as Uz. He was one to always avoid evil. Satan challenged God to let him punish him because Satan believed that he would give up on God. Job was afflicted with diseases, loss of wealth, and much more. He was encouraged to curse God, but didn't. He remained faithful to God. His friends tormented him. He was thrown everything in the book. His friends blamed him for his shortcomings, as if he had done something wrong. And when Job could have given up, he defended the people about how great God was despite his current situation. He overcame what Satan had thrown at him, even when it was hard, and God restored his wealth, health, and everything else* (***Job 1 –paraphrase***). My dad and I talked about this, and we understood that no matter what it looked like, it was in God's plan. At that moment, an everlasting memory was recorded in my brain. My dad and I had a heart to heart that led us to God. This was the first time in a very long time that we were that close. Our relationship was flourishing, and at that time, God used me to calm my dad's storm. I listened to God, and He told me exactly what to do and what to say. This was part of igniting my purpose in God. God had a plan that allowed me to go through that relationship struggle with my dad to lead us to better circumstances. We were ministering to each other, and we were putting God at the forefront of the situation. Sure, it was hard watching my dad not be able to breathe. It was hard being at the hospital three to four times a week. It was hard on our whole family, but we were listening to the voice of God. We listened and remained faithful to God regardless of the circumstance. These were tests. These were times where God grew me spiritually. He was preparing me for what was to come.

During these times, He allowed me to minister to my dad. He allowed my dad to minister to me. These were some broken areas where we were both growing. This was necessary in my journey. Everything we go through eventually plays a role in our purpose. Think about the people whose lives changed because of your spiritual obedience to God's call on your life. What if you hadn't listened? We all go through things that allow God to take us right where we need to be. In the beginning of the book, I mentioned that my dad's love was ostracized from me. We spent time apart, but now I was ministering to him, and he was ministering to me. It was a shift through God. Can you imagine the chains that were broken? It was spiritual. The trials at the beginning birthed strength for the purpose that God intended to happen. I needed that closure. I needed that relationship healed before God could bless me with someone that I could grow to love. There was a void that God was intentionally filling, and it was about timing. Everything was connected. That's how God works. When we feel like our journey through the pain and the process is not working, we must learn to still trust God. I didn't understand why the man that I was dating fit perfectly with my list, but couldn't connect with me. I now realized *that situation wasn't for me.* God was grooming who He had prepared for me, but there were also trials and tribulations that needed to be overcome in my life before God thought I was ready. I wasn't prepared for who was preparing for me. Has God ever told you to do something and you didn't? When that happens, we miss the opportunities like this for God to use us. God used me in this situation with my dad. The decisions that I made through my journey were aligning with my purpose and that was important. It changed the trajectory of what was to come next. When we get aligned with the will of God, God shifts things into gear for the outcome He wants, not for the outcome we want.

Nevertheless, this was a trial that was making me stronger. This was a trial that had bettered me as a person. I knew that my faith had stretched. I knew that my life was changing, and God knew what was happening. I had a friend that was literally just a friend, nothing more. I had been communicating with him for business. Our conversations never went beyond trading. He was an awesome trader, and he was teaching me to trade as an investor. We would talk on the phone during the trades and get off the phone when it was done. That was it. It was all business related. One day I decided to drive to Alabama for one of the live trade meetings that our trading group was having. It was the first time that I saw him in person. We had a friendly conversation about trading, and what to do from there with the opportunity. When I got in my car that day, *God said he was the one that He was preparing for me.* I literally laughed at God. It was hilarious. I didn't know anything about this guy, and I thought I heard wrong. I didn't say anything, and I didn't do anything about it. I told God he would have to show me that he was for me.

Months later, we had an event in Georgia where I live. There was nothing different from the last time we talked. We got along. He was a cool person, but that was it. That was the extent of it. I was minding my business, not even focused on what God told me. We were talking to a lady during the meeting, and she asked if we were married. We laughed. She said that we just looked like we were married. We looked like a couple. Again, we laughed it off. When I got home, I thought God was playing with me. I literally was laughing. I could name a million things that screamed he wasn't my type, but that's how God works. When we begin to walk the walk that God has for us, we gain spiritual guidance. God continually sent me guidance in every area of my life. God would give me a peek into my future, and I had to trust that He had it under control. After the lady mentioned the comment about being married, I didn't mention it to God anymore. It seems as if He kept sending confirmations, but I didn't act on them. Honestly, I didn't believe them. This guy wasn't anything that I asked for, but God would slowly continue to communicate with me.

One weekend, the guy texted me and said that he was in town. He didn't live in Georgia, so he would occasionally tell me if he came to my area. I didn't think too much into it. I was with one of my close friends and her mom at the time, and I was telling them that this guy that I was doing business with told me he was going to be in town. My friend's mom asked if he was someone I was interested in dating, and I said no, he's just a friend. I was laughing about it. It still hadn't really sunk in. I didn't believe what God was telling me. We had never shown interest in each other. We just stayed in touch since the last event. It was just a casual friendship. That weekend, we never even got together because my dad was in the hospital, and I was really focused on seeing him and spending time with him. I did explain that to the guy, and from that point on, he would occasionally check on me to see how my dad was doing. That was our friendship, nothing more and nothing less. However, when I was working in Texas, God made things very evident, and there was a shift that took place. One conversation that started off about trading ended up being almost five hours. Then, it happened the next day, and the next, and the next. Two weeks went by from us talking and having long conversations that never got boring. We were intrigued with each other, beyond just trading. It was evident that this relationship had potential beyond a friendship. However, I was still reserved. When I got back to Georgia, he was supposed to drive to Georgia and take me on a date. I can remember conversations with my friends before our first date, and I just didn't know if this guy could really be the one for me. He was not the perfect guy from my checklist, but I would later find out that he was perfect for me. After the first date, I knew what God had told me was the truth.

A true friendship was formed. I knew it was God. It felt right. It all aligned. Our conversations even our arguments led to growth. When we first starting dating, my dad was still in and out of the hospital. He was there for me when I needed a friend the most. I know God did that. I had a friend, a real friend. He courted me during one of the most heartbreaking times of my life. In April of 2016, when we first began to go on dates, my dad was getting worse. It had gotten to the point that he had no choice but to get a heart surgery. He was on the heart transplant list, but no heart had come through yet. He was going to have to get a fake heart, an LVAD. My dad didn't want it. He didn't want an electronic heart, and I was a wreck. I was crying almost every day, and it was a challenging time for my family. It was a difficult for me to be dating someone, but God gave me peace about this guy. He prayed for my dad. He kept me uplifted so that I could have the strength to smile at my daddy every day and tell him that it was going to be okay. This is how God works. He orchestrated the help when He knew I would need it. God knew I would value the help during this time. I knew I was walking the path God intended for me. I knew I was at my purpose. I needed to be there for my dad, and He gave me someone to be there for me. Many nights I prayed for my dad to change his mind about the surgery, and many days my family prayed together. There were many days my guy and I would pray. Many days my best friend and I would pray. God ordained the right people to be around me. This was part of the reason God removed certain people, and God retained certain people. It was for this time.

I remember one day when I was back at work, I got a call saying that my dad needed to have emergency surgery. I was out of town, and my dad's heart had failed. He didn't have a choice now. If he wanted to live, he had to get the LVAD surgery, and he decided that he would give life another chance. I remember the long day waiting for the doctors to give an update on my dad. I was waiting on the phone call, but the whole time, I had someone in my corner looking out for me. God was working. It was a support circle. I prayed and prayed and we prayed and prayed, and eventually news came back that my dad's surgery went well. Things were looking up from here. Things were going to get better. This LVAD was going to prolong my dad's life for ten years. This was God. It was a miracle. I was thankful for everything that happened during that time. My dad's life was extended, and God had given me a guy that stood by me in trying times. It wasn't easy to date me, but he was created for me, and God was showing me that He had a plan the entire time.

The amazing thing about it is that I heard from God many months before this moment manifested. My mind wasn't even ready to receive it. God gave me what He knew I needed when He wanted me to have it. He was the total opposite of everything on my checklist. Of course, he does love God, but he had two kids, was divorced, ten years older than me, and from a totally different state, but he was who God wanted for me. God showed me in our first three months of going on dates. God showed me with my own eyes that I was where I was supposed to be. Within 3 months, we were officially dating, and I was meeting his children, family, friends, and he was meeting mine. It was so special because he was praying for my dad before they met. The first time my dad met him, they became instantly connected. It was nothing but God. I thought my parents would be a little upset about his tenure, children, and past situation, but they embraced him. They loved him from the beginning. From the very first day, my dad approved of him, and that wasn't easy to do. The way it all fell into place was amazing. His family loved me. His kids loved me. Our friends loved us together. It was nothing negative I could say. Again, we weren't perfect, but we were with who God intended for us to be with. We listened. We obeyed. We went through the process, and we were on the path towards our purpose.

Everything was great. Everyone got along. It was the happiest I had ever been in my life. He was helping me grow, and I was helping him get over past hurt. It was given by God. He respected my choice of celibacy. He embraced it. He waits on me. He was everything God wanted for me, and everything I had gone through during my process was leading me to where I needed to be. God knew my match. God knew who was for me. I was at a point in my life where God's path for my life was unveiling itself. God was building up what was for me. My pain, my process, my purpose was beginning to be revealed and I was at a point where God was in total control of my life. If I wouldn't have listened to God, then my journey to getting to this relationship would have been much longer. I learned to listen to God to guide me. Everything that was in my past birthed something in me so that God could bless me with who He prepared for me. I didn't understand why I had to go through the relationship I went through. Although I chose that path, there was something that God taught me through the journey, and it was needed through my process. I didn't know why God asked me to be celibate, but now I understood what the process taught me. I was walking into my purpose, and everything was in alignment.

Chapter 12:
Aligning my Purpose with my Spiritual Identity

Think about a time in your life where you listened to God and everything began to align. When we reach a point with God where we are in sync with Him, we are at a place where He can use us for the things in which we were designed. This relationship was confirmation from God that I was on the right track. For the first time in my life, everything was beginning to align itself. There were imperfect things in my life, but it didn't matter. I knew that God had a plan for me. I knew that I was walking in His will. I knew that I was walking through the purpose that He had designed for me. Our purpose is tied to our spiritual identities. At the beginning of the book, I mentioned that I was lost. I didn't know who I was. I didn't understand myself. I didn't understand love. I didn't understand anything. At that point in my life, the devil had full control of me. He controlled my thoughts of myself, and he had a goal to destroy the plan that God intended for my life. However, through the pain of my choices, God created a process for me to go through to find myself IN HIM. This was the journey of discovering my spiritual identity. As I began to find myself, God made me whole. He filled the voids that were created by everything that I went through in my life. As the voids began to fill, He began to birth my purpose. This is where my life turned around, and it's where your life will begin to turn around as well. Once we find who we are in God, then God begins to reveal the plan that He has for us. He begins to align the correct relationships, friendships, and situations to push us to where we need to be in Him. This relationship was a stepping stone of the steps I was taking towards my purpose.

The relationship gave me a person that taught me, not a love that completed me, but a love that worked with me. It was a companionship. God gave me someone that would help build me up as a person. God prepared me for celibacy, so that the relationship that He gave me would be pure. He gave me a person that would be understanding, loving, patient, kind, respectful, and so much more. He would be ready to assist me through every trial and tribulation. God was preparing him specifically for the things He knew I would encounter on my journey, and He was specifically preparing me for the things he would face on his journey. My list was nonexistent when it came to the man that God gave me. Waiting for God is so important. I thought I knew what I wanted, but God knew what I needed. God knew the pain I went through. God knew the process I had to go through, and God knew the purpose that was intended for me. He knew what I would soon encounter, and it was majestically orchestrated by God.

Everything was going great. I was happy. My happiness was not defined by my relationship, but my happiness came from the journey that God had taken me through and the blessings that He gave me. However, along with those blessing still came trials. God perfectly arranged them, and I was getting ready to face the biggest trial of my life. Our relationship was going great. My dad was healthy again. He was driving. He was moving. He was having longer conversations. Life was great.

PAIN. PROCESS. PURPOSE.

One day, October 6th to be exact, I went to visit my dad. He seemed very tired, but we had a great conversation. We laughed. We enjoyed ourselves. We watched videos of my goddaughter from her birthday party, and we even talked to my boyfriend on the phone. I remember the conversation after my boyfriend hung up was that he really liked him. He knew that he was the one for me. I remember the details of our conversation, and the approvals he had given me. We also began to watch a movie until he started dozing off. It was a good day. However, when I first got there I was little distracted because of the commotion of a tornado possibly coming through our city, and my mom being overdramatic because she was out of town. I remember that day. I left to go shopping after about two or three hours, and I told my dad I loved him and when I left the outlets I'd come back to see him. When I walked out the door, God told me to go back and talk to my dad, I didn't. When I got to the front gate of the neighborhood, I heard God tell me again, I didn't go. When I got to the highway, God told me to turn around and I got stuck in traffic. I'll never forget that day. The next day, I tried to call my dad over fifty times, but there was no answer. I went back to the house, and I found him on his bedroom floor. He had gone to be with the Lord. My dad had passed away. That was a very difficult day for me. Everything that we had progressed to through our process was gone. Our relationship had just mended, and he wasn't here anymore. I thought he had another ten years, but it wasn't in God's plan. I didn't know how to accept that.

My world ended for a moment that day. I literally was numb. I called my boyfriend, my best friends, and then one of my close friends, and no words could really be formulated. I was sitting with my dad's body. Police were coming in the house, and I couldn't do anything. That day seemed unreal, but I made it through. The next weeks were also difficult, but I made it through. What came next was what the devil thought would break me. When my dad passed, I thought it was my fault. It was a defining moment in my relationship with God. I disobeyed, and I missed a moment that I had to remember forever. I continued to try to beat myself up about not turning around and not going to talk to my dad. That was eating me alive. I didn't know what to do. The way I felt was unexplainable. What God had to show me was that regardless of my obedience or disobedience, it was my dad's time. When I didn't turn around, I couldn't have changed anything about his outcome, I could have only changed our last moments. It wasn't my fault, even though I felt it was. I had to learn that this was a part of my process. For the next three months, I had many up and down days, but this is where I realized that God perfectly orchestrated everything. He still had my best interest in mind throughout the entire process. During that time, I had a companion that was patient and prayerful. I had the circle of friends that prayed and supported. When I wanted to give up on God for taking my dad away, they wouldn't let me. When I wanted to blame myself, they wouldn't let me. God knew what was coming, and He orchestrated a team of people to be there for me. He knew what I would need, and He knew the strength He would build in me from this. This period ignited my purpose.

I told the story about my dad because it played a significant role in my purpose. As I mentioned, I blamed myself for my disobedience, and I couldn't tell you what me turning around would have changed, but I know that what God intended for my dad was going to happen. However, that lesson was the defining moment in me. I learned that God will give us chances through our spiritual journey to make wise decisions, and even when we don't make the decision He wants us to, He births a lesson through the path we choose to take. Everything created a full circle of purpose. At the beginning of the book, I told you the broken relationship that my dad and I had. We didn't talk for almost a year, and that was a very long time for me. He hurt me, and I hurt him. We didn't know how to communicate. At some life defining moments, we went through some emotional times, but God began to heal us both. Eventually, when we did come back to each other, I was able to minister to him, and God used me. Our relationship grew, and we had better conversations than we ever had. He allowed our relationship to come full circle. He allowed our voids to be filled. He redesigned our relationship at the time where it made the biggest impact to the both of us. My dad had always been there in my life, and the time we separated hurt us. However, God allowed the relationship to grow to a different level, and all the pain made our bond stronger. When my dad passed, I blamed myself. I was infuriated that I didn't listen to God, but there was still a blessing in the lesson. In the same breath, I wanted to blame myself, but I realized that God had used me again in my dad's life. I even had to acknowledge that I was the very last person who God allowed my dad to have a conversation with. He used me as the last vessel of communication to any human that my dad had on this earth. His last spent moments were with me. His last conversations were with me. I was given the opportunity to live in those last moments. My dad left this earth after we were at peace. I was a vital part of him, and I was the last piece of his journey. God knew that would happen, and He perfectly orchestrated the process. That was a blessing and an honor. Not only was I the last conversation, He used me to find my dad the next day and be the strength of the family for my mom and brother. As vulnerable as my heart was, God gave me the strength to be able to take on that task, and to do it in a manner that respected my dad. Even though I didn't listen the night before he passed when I was told to turn around, in this moment, I was able to make a difference in the situation. That was part of my purpose. I had to decide to use my optimistic mind to find God's Will in the situation. This birthed a strength that I didn't know I had. This changed me.

My purpose was now defined by a journey that I took with God, and I was left with a purpose. I want to take this time to encourage anyone reading this book that has lost a parent or spouse to find God in the moments that you did have. God turned a dark time in my dad and I's relationship into something far greater than what we had. He has left me with so many great and vital memories that will allow his legacy to live forever. I'm thankful for that. Although death is such a challenging thing to deal with, remember that God will allow everything to come full circle. Every life defining thing that happens in your life will birth something for your future. Nothing is ever done by God in vain. It was my dad's time, but God made sure he fulfilled his purpose in life before he left. My dad touched thousands of men during his time here on earth. He had his own spiritual journey, and he went through it well. In his 56 years on this earth, he impacted many young men. There are men that consistently tell me the impact my dad had on their life was ever lasting. The torch had been passed. It was my turn to create that legacy. I knew that God was preparing me to be a light like my dad was. My purpose was given to me through pain and a process, and God showed me what I'm supposed to do in life. My purpose is to touch as many women through God as possible. **My pain produced strength. My lost identity allowed me to search for God, and allow him to make me whole. My loss of love produced a healthy relationship blessed by God. My process birthed the purpose.**

Sometimes, when we go through life, we never realize how the dots connect. Every person that we meet will eventually circle around. Every decision that we make will be connected to something else God has for us. What I've learned is that God will allow us to go through things to birth something new within us. Through my journey, I felt as if God birthed a new identity for me. At the beginning, I was masked. I was afraid of me. I didn't know who I was, but God held my hand, and showed me that He was with me. I wasn't defined by my mistakes that I made in the past. I learned from them. God took what the devil wanted to make bad, and He made it good. I got off track, but I learned how to get back on track. I lost people, but I gained God ordained friendships. My father went to be with God, but through that I birthed strength and purpose. I didn't value myself or know what love was, but I found love through God to learn to love myself. Then, God blessed me with a man He prepared for me. God had a plan all along. The decisions that we make along the path may detour us for a moment, but we can always get back on track with God. I encourage every person reading this book to look at your journey. Don't give up. Don't allow the devil to take control of you. Have patience during your process. Spend some time alone, and find out what God is preparing you for because God has a plan. I found out God's plan for my life after a series of events and one traumatic event that pushed me to where I needed to be. It put me in a place completely and totally with God. I will make mistakes, and I may not always know the right thing to do, but I do know that God will always be with me. I will never feel alone because He will always be by my side showing me how to live out the purpose He has preordained for my life. He will do the same for you. He will give you a purpose to live on this earth for. I don't know what stage of the process you may be in, but I will tell you that your spiritual identity is birthed within your purpose. I hope you have learned something through my journey. You may encounter pain, but there will be that process that strengthens you and teaches you to be who God needs you to be. Throughout that process to your spiritual identity you will birth PURPOSE, and God will continue to guide you along the way!

PAIN . PROCESS . PURPOSE .

Your Intimate Thoughts

Here's a section where I want you all to reflect on your God given *purpose*. Take some time and allow God to tell you exactly what His Plan is for your life. I will leave you some space to write.

Love Always,

Chanel

_____
_____
_____
_____
_____
_____
_____
_____
_____
_____
_____
_____
_____
_____
_____
_____
_____
_____

PAIN. PROCESS. PURPOSE.

PAIN. PROCESS. PURPOSE.

PAIN. PROCESS. PURPOSE.

There is a workbook that is a companion to this book. If you have the workbook, I give you specific questions to answer and exercises to complete after you've finished the book to help you with your process. I hope that my journey can impact the life of every person that picks up this book. I pray that you grow closer to God, and you realize that nothing in your life is too hard for God to fix. All things are possible to those that believe.

God Bless and Enjoy!

PAIN
PROCESS
PURPOSE:
THE 3 P'S TO FINDING YOUR SPIRITUAL IDENTITY

Chanel L. Chase

Let's Keep in Contact

Website: www.pain2purposebook.com

@pain2purposebook

Page: fb.me/pain2purposebook
Group: **Pain Process Purpose**

pain2purposebk

info@pain2purposebook.com

Book Me for Your Next Event:
info@chanelchase.com
www.chanelchase.com

Please send me a pic on Instagram or Facebook with you holding your book copy. Message me and let me know how you enjoyed the book and I would love to hear about your personal journey if you feel you want to share. I would love to hear the impact that my journey had on your life. We are sisters, and we are working together to reach our God intended journeys together!

Love Always,

Chanel

About the Author

Chanel Chase is a take charge business woman, author, and inspirational speaker who expertly balances career, ministry, and family. She is a voice to the millennials and the Kingdom of God. Chanel has received many honors, including graduating Valedictorian of Miles College in 2012, and many other accolades such as appearing on the Steve Harvey Show, writing for Ntwrkr Magazine, and becoming an established 6 figure earner, while juggling life in corporate America and entrepreneurship. She is a true believer that God wants everyone to succeed. She is a passionate, take charge, self-motivated, powerful strategic thinker raised in the suburbs of Atlanta and is dedicated to inspiring women to embark on their own spiritual journey and live in their purpose.

PAIN.PROCESS.PURPOSE.

CHANEL CHASE

PAIN.PROCESS.PURPOSE.

CHANEL CHASE

PAIN. PROCESS. PURPOSE.

CHANEL CHASE

www.ingramcontent.com/pod-product-compliance
Lightning Source LLC
Chambersburg PA
CBHW070457100426
42743CB00010B/1661